Children's Songs

ISBN 978-1-4950-1984-5

cherry lane
music company

EXCLUSIVELY DISTRIBUTED BY

HAL•LEONARD®
CORPORATION
7777 W. BLUEMOUND RD. P.O. BOX 13819 MILWAUKEE, WI 53213

For all works contained herein:
Unauthorized copying, arranging, adapting, recording, Internet posting, public performance,
or other distribution of the printed music in this publication is an infringement of copyright.

CONTENTS

ADDAMS FAMILY THEME
Theme from the TV Show and Movie

Music and Lyrics by
VIC MIZZY

They're creep-y and they're kook-y, mys-te-ri-ous and spook-y, they're al-to-geth-er ook-y, the Ad-dams Fam-i-ly. Their house is a mu-se-um, where

Copyright © 1964, Renewed 1992 by Unison Music Company
Administered by Next Decade Entertainment, Inc.
International Copyright Secured   All Rights Reserved

A-TISKET A-TASKET

Traditional

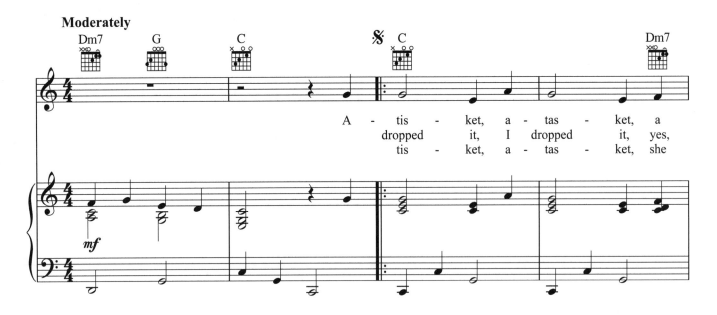

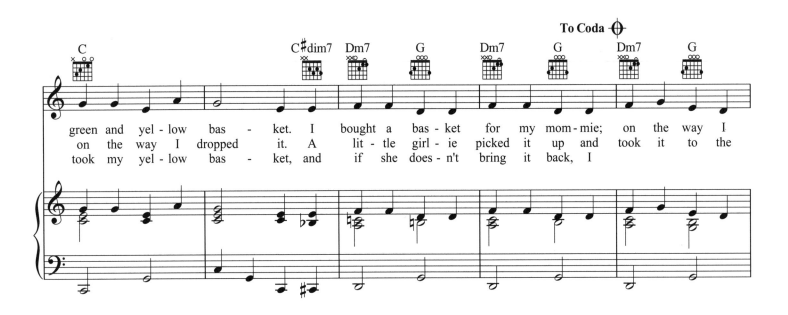

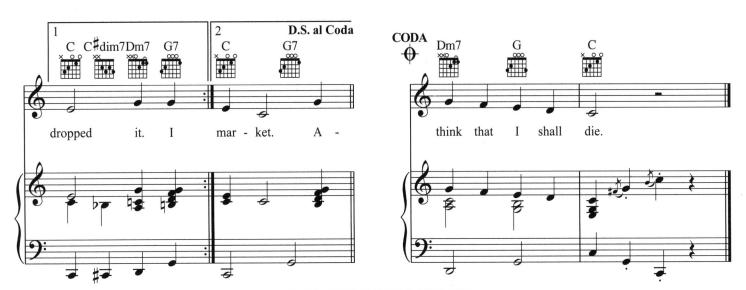

Copyright © 2000 by HAL LEONARD CORPORATION
International Copyright Secured   All Rights Reserved

AMAZING GRACE

Words by JOHN NEWTON
Traditional American Melody

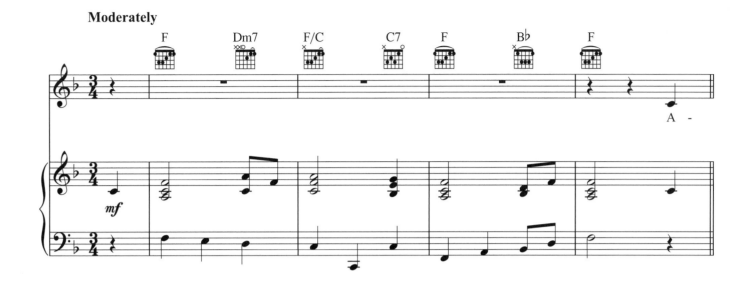

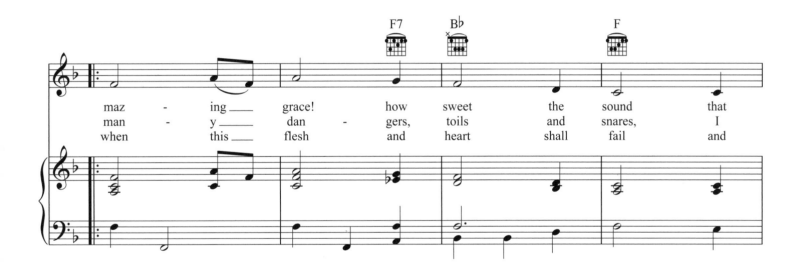

Copyright © 2001 by HAL LEONARD CORPORATION
International Copyright Secured   All Rights Reserved

lost, but now _____ am _____ found, was blind, but _____
brought me safe _____ thus _____ far, and grace will _____
sess with - in _____ the _____ veil a life of _____

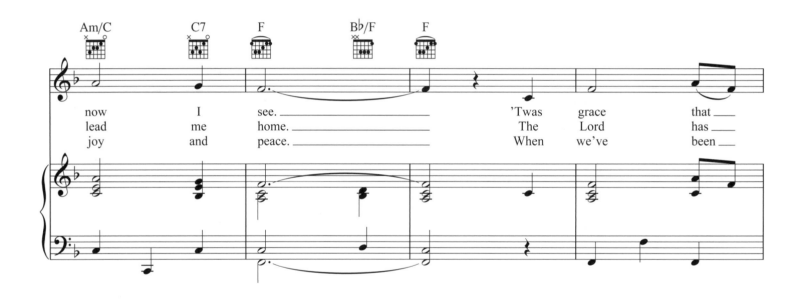

now I see. _____ 'Twas grace that _____
lead me home. _____ The Lord has _____
joy and peace. _____ When we've been _____

taught my heart to fear, and grace my _____
prom - ised good to me, His word my _____
there ten thou - sand years, bright shin - ing _____

fears re - lieved._____ How pre - cious ___
hope se - cures._____ He will _____ my ___
as the ___ sun,_____ we've no _____ less ___

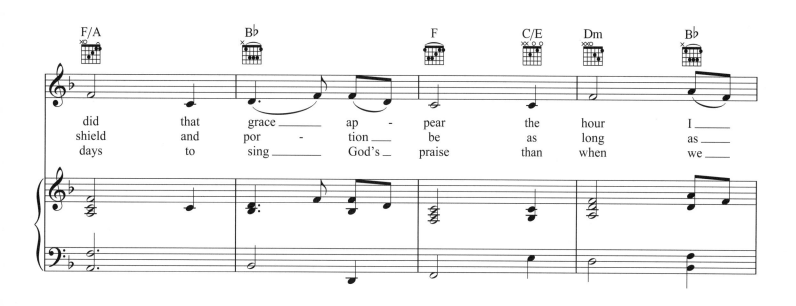

did that grace ___ ap - pear the hour I ___
shield and por - tion ___ be as long as ___
days to sing ___ God's ___ praise than when we ___

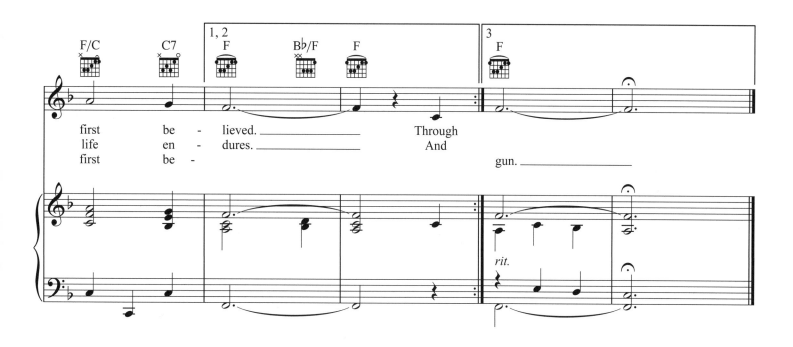

first be - lieved._____ Through
life en - dures._____ And
first be -
gun._____

rit.

AMERICA, THE BEAUTIFUL

Words by KATHERINE LEE BATES
Music by SAMUEL A. WARD

1. O beau - ti - ful for spa - cious skies, for am - ber waves of
2. beau - ti - ful for pil - grim feet, whose stern, im - pas - sioned
3.,4. *(See additional verses)*

grain, for pur - ple moun - tain maj - es - ties a - bove the fruit - ed
stress, a thor - ough - fare for free - dom beat a - cross the wil - der -

plain! A - mer - i - ca! A - mer - i - ca! God shed His grace on
ness! A - mer - i - ca! A - mer - i - ca! God mend thine ev - ery

Copyright © 1991 by HAL LEONARD CORPORATION
International Copyright Secured   All Rights Reserved

Additional Verses

3. O beautiful for heroes proved
   In liberating strife,
   Who more than self their country loved
   And mercy more than life!
   America! America!
   May God thy gold refine
   'Til all success be nobleness
   And every gain divine.

4. O beautiful for patriot dream
   That sees beyond the years;
   Thine alabaster cities gleam
   Undimmed by human tears.
   America! America!
   God shed His grace on thee,
   And crown thy good with brotherhood,
   From sea to shining sea.

ANCHORS AWEIGH

Words by ALFRED HART MILES and ROYAL LOVELL
Music by CHARLES A. ZIMMERMAN
Additional Lyric by GEORGE D. LOTTMAN

Bright March tempo

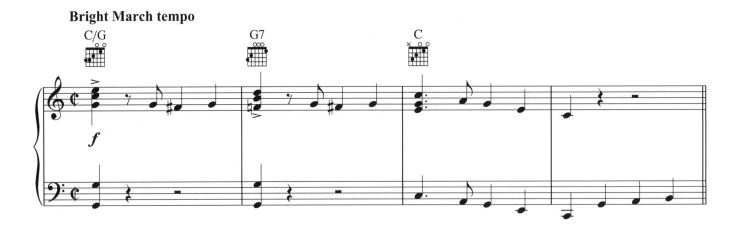

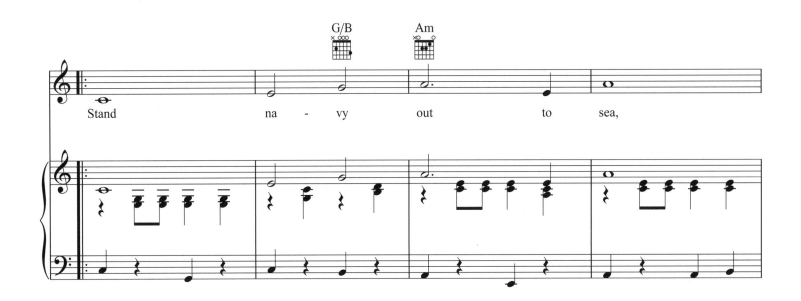

Stand na - vy out to sea,

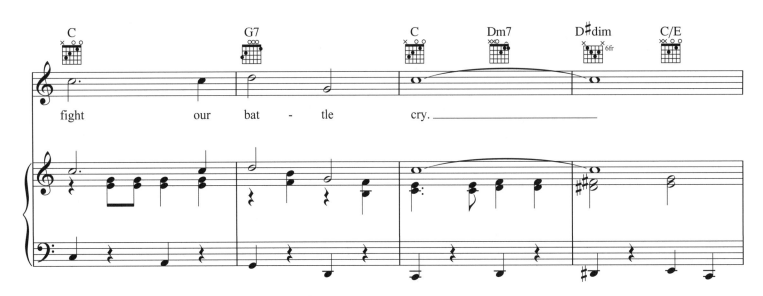

fight our bat - tle cry. _____

Copyright © 1991 by HAL LEONARD CORPORATION
International Copyright Secured   All Rights Reserved

ANY DREAM WILL DO

from JOSEPH AND THE AMAZING TECHNICOLOR® DREAMCOAT

Music by ANDREW LLOYD WEBBER
Lyrics by TIM RICE

© Copyright 1969 The Really Useful Group Ltd.
Copyright Renewed
International Copyright Secured   All Rights Reserved

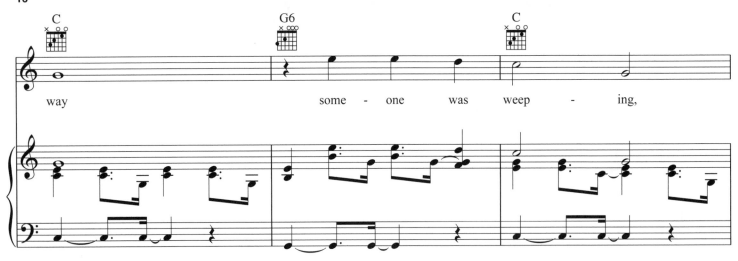

way some - one was weep - ing,

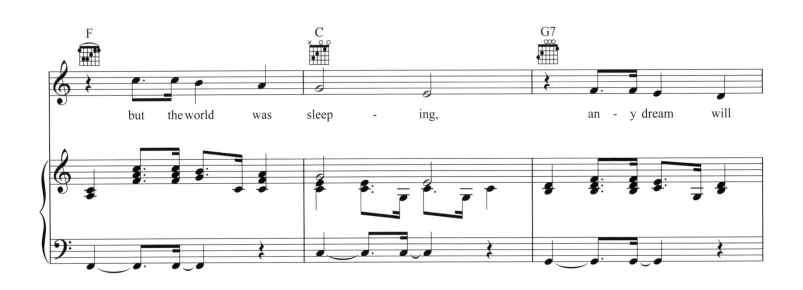

but the world was sleep - ing, an - y dream will

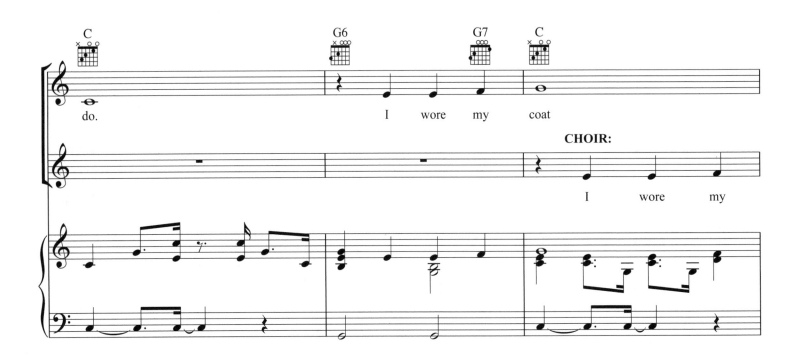

do.

I wore my coat

CHOIR:

I wore my

BATTLE HYMN OF THE REPUBLIC

Words by JULIA WARD HOWE
Music by WILLIAM STEFFE

1. Mine eyes have seen the glo-ry of the com-ing of the Lord. He is
2. seen him in the watch-fires of the hun-dred cir-cling camps. They have
3.–5. *(See additional verses)*

tram-pling out the vin-tage where the grapes of wrath are stored. He hath
build-ed Him an al-tar in the eve-ning dews and damps. I have

loos'd the fate-ful light-ning of His ter-ri-ble swift sword. His
read His right-eous sen-tence by the dim and flar-ing lamps. His

Copyright © 1995 by HAL LEONARD CORPORATION
International Copyright Secured   All Rights Reserved

Additional Verses

3. I have read a fiery gospel writ in burnished rows of steel.
   As ye deal with my contempters, so with you my grace shall deal.
   Let the hero born of woman crush the serpent with his heel,
   Since God is marching on.

4. He has sounded forth the trumpet that shall never call retreat.
   He is sifting out the hearts of men before His judgement seat.
   O be swift, my soul, to answer Him, be jubilant, my feet.
   Our God is marching on.

5. In the beauty of the lilies, Christ was born across the sea
   With a glory in His bosom that transfigures you and me.
   As He died to make men holy, let us die to make men free,
   While God is marching on.

BE OUR GUEST
from Walt Disney's BEAUTY AND THE BEAST

Music by ALAN MENKEN
Lyrics by HOWARD ASHMAN

LUMIERE: *Ma chère Mademoiselle! It is with deepest pride and greatest pleasure that*

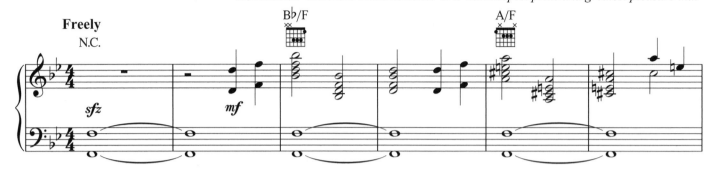

we welcome you here tonight. And now, we invite you to relax. Let us pull up a chair as the dining room proudly presents...

Moderate 2, unhurried

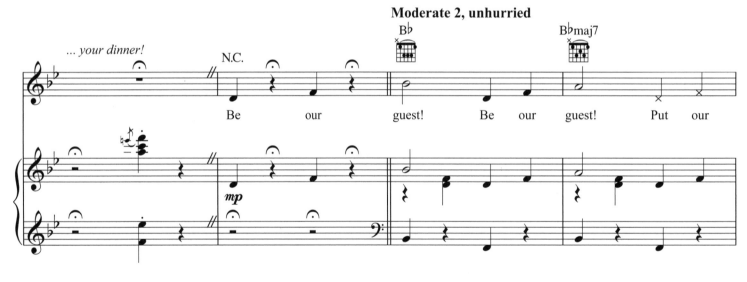

... your dinner!

Be our guest! Be our guest! Put our

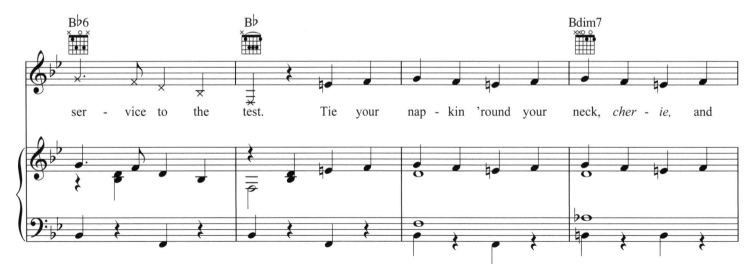

ser - vice to the test. Tie your nap - kin 'round your neck, *cher - ie,* and

© 1991 Walt Disney Music Company and Wonderland Music Company, Inc.
All Rights Reserved   Used by Permission

LUMIERE: bet. _____ Come on and lift your glass. _____ You've won your

own free pass _____ to be our guest. **LUMIERE:** If you're stressed, it's fine

din-ing we sug-gest. **CHORUS:** Be our guest! Be our guest! Be our

Grandly – same tempo

guest! _____

guest! Be our guest! _____

Ah _____

mf *increase gradually*

Ah _____

ff

Slower, morosely

LUMIERE:
Life is so un - nerv - ing for a ser - vant who's not serv - ing. He's not whole with - out a soul to wait up - on. Ah, those good old days when we were use - ful... Sud - den - ly those good old days are

BELIEVE

from Warner Bros. Pictures' THE POLAR EXPRESS

Words and Music by GLEN BALLARD
and ALAN SILVESTRI

Chil - dren ___ sleep - ing, ___ snow is soft - ly
Trains move ___ quick - ly ___ to their jour - ney's

fall - ing. ___ Dreams are call - ing ___
end. Des - ti - na - tions ___

like bells in ___ the dis - tance.
are where we ___ be - gin a - gain.

Copyright © 2004 Joblana Music, Universal Music Corp., Hazen Music and Arlovol Music
All Rights on behalf of Joblana Music Administered by Sony/ATV Music Publishing LLC, 424 Church Street, Suite 1200, Nashville, TN 37219
All Rights on behalf of Hazen Music Administered by Universal Music Corp.
All Rights on behalf of Arlovol Music Administered by Penny Farthing Music c/o The Bicycle Music Company
International Copyright Secured All Rights Reserved

THE BIBLE TELLS ME SO

Words and Music by
DALE EVANS

Copyright © 1955 Roy Rogers Music
Copyright Renewed
All Rights Administered by Sony/ATV Music Publishing LLC, 424 Church Street, Suite 1200, Nashville, TN 37219
International Copyright Secured   All Rights Reserved

BUNNY HOP

Words and Music by RAY ANTHONY
and LEONARD AULETTI

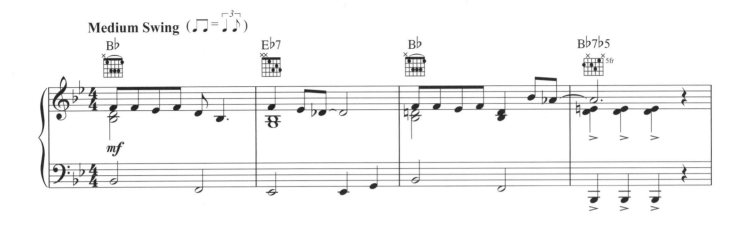

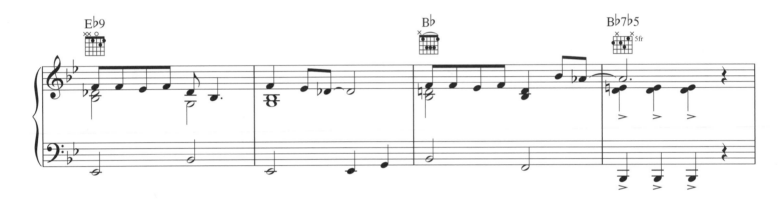

Copyright © 1952 Moonlight Music, Inc.
Copyright Renewed
All Rights Reserved   Used by Permission

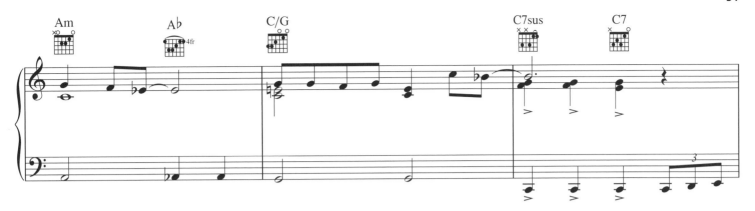

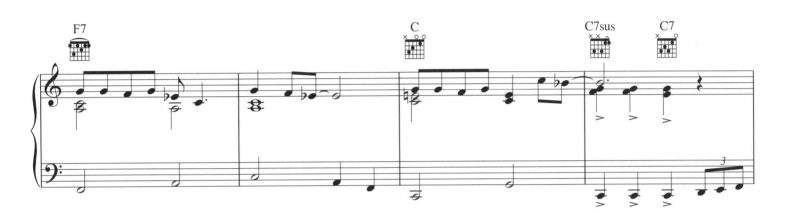

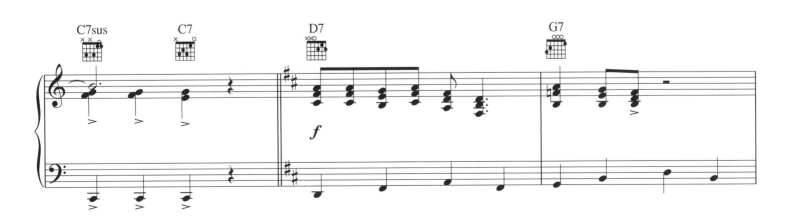

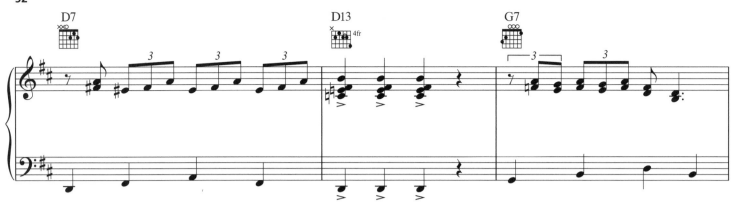

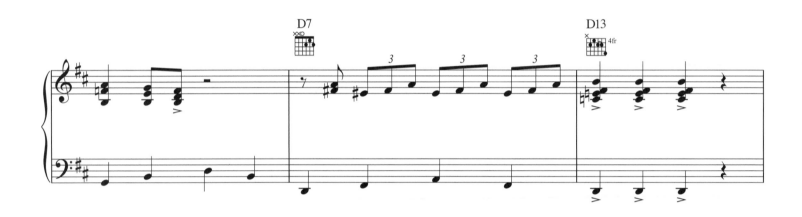

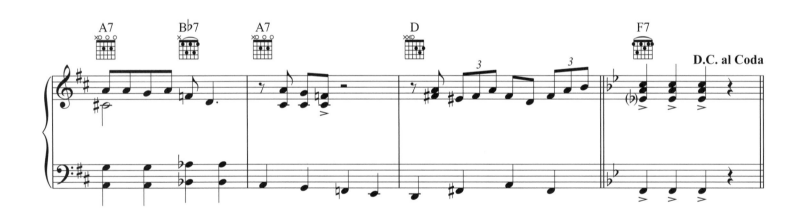

THE CAISSONS GO ROLLING ALONG

Words and Music by
EDMUND L. GRUBER

Copyright © 1991 by HAL LEONARD CORPORATION
International Copyright Secured   All Rights Reserved

CASTLE ON A CLOUD
from LES MISÉRABLES

Music by CLAUDE-MICHEL SCHÖNBERG
Lyrics by ALAIN BOUBLIL, JEAN-MARC NATEL
and HERBERT KRETZMER

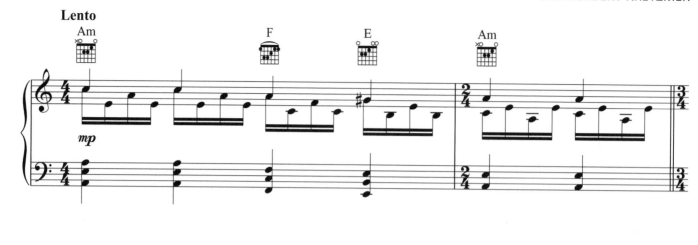

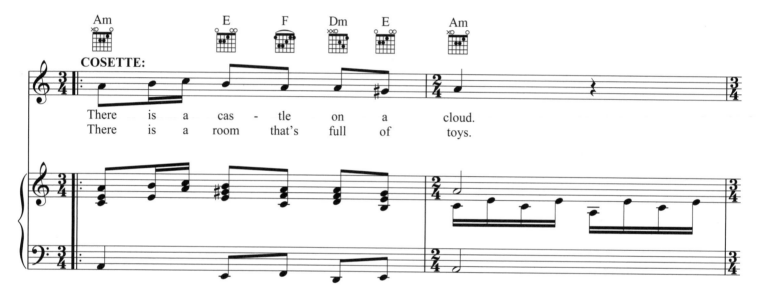

Music and Lyrics Copyright © 1980 by Editions Musicales Alain Boublil
English Lyrics Copyright © 1986 by Alain Boublil Music Ltd. (ASCAP)
Mechanical and Publication Rights for the U.S.A. Administered by Alain Boublil Music Ltd. (ASCAP) c/o Joel Faden & Co., Inc.,
MLM 250 West 57th St., 26th Floor, New York, NY 10107, Tel. (212) 246-7203, Fax (212) 246-7217, jfaden@joelfaden.com
International Copyright Secured. All Rights Reserved. This music is copyright. Photocopying is illegal.
All Performance Rights Restricted.

THE CHICKEN DANCE

By TERRY RENDALL
and WERNER THOMAS
English Lyrics by PAUL PARNES

Copyright © 1972, 1974 by Intervox Music, Kontich, Belgium
Copyright Renewed
All Rights for the U.S.A. and Canada Controlled by September Music Corp., 421 Seventh Avenue, New York, NY 10001
International Copyright Secured   All Rights Reserved

Additional Lyrics

2. Hey, you're in the swing.
   You're cluckin' like a bird. (Pluck, pluck, pluck, pluck.)
   You're flappin' your wings.
   Don't you feel absurd. (No, no, no, no.)
   It's a chicken dance,
   Like a rooster and a hen. (Ya, ya, ya, ya.)
   Flappy chicken dance;
   Let's do it again. *(To Chorus 2:)*

Chorus 2:
   Relax and let the music move you.
   Let all your inhibitions go.
   Just watch your partner whirl around you.
   We're havin' fun now; I told you so.

3. Now you're flappin' like a bird
   And you're wigglin' too. (I like that move.)
   You're without a care.
   It's a dance for you. (Just made for you.)
   Keep doin' what you do.
   Don't you cop out now. (Don't cop out now.)
   Gets better as you dance;
   Catch your breath somehow.
   Chorus

4. Now we're almost through,
   Really flyin' high. (Bye, bye, bye, bye.)
   All you chickens and birds,
   Time to say goodbye. (To say goodbye.)
   Goin' back to the nest,
   But the flyin' was fun. (Oh, it was fun.)
   Chicken dance was the best,
   But the dance is done.

COLORS OF THE WIND

from Walt Disney's POCAHONTAS

Music by ALAN MENKEN
Lyrics by STEPHEN SCHWARTZ

© 1995 Wonderland Music Company, Inc. and Walt Disney Music Company
All Rights Reserved   Used by Permission

CHITTY CHITTY BANG BANG

from the Motion Picture CHITTY CHITTY BANG BANG

Words and Music by RICHARD M. SHERMAN
and ROBERT B. SHERMAN

© 1968 (Renewed) EMI UNART CATALOG INC.
All Rights Administered by EMI UNART CATALOG INC. (Publishing) and ALFRED MUSIC (Print)
All Rights Reserved   Used by Permission

CIRCLE OF LIFE
from Walt Disney Pictures' THE LION KING

Music by ELTON JOHN
Lyrics by TIM RICE

© 1994 Wonderland Music Company, Inc.
All Rights Reserved   Used by Permission

cir - cle, _____ the cir - cle ___ of life.

DING-DONG! THE WITCH IS DEAD

from THE WIZARD OF OZ

Lyric by E.Y. "YIP" HARBURG
Music by HAROLD ARLEN

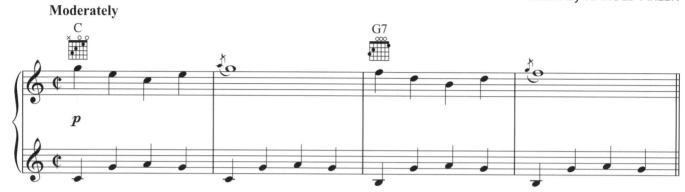

Once there was a wick-ed witch in the love-ly land of Oz, and a

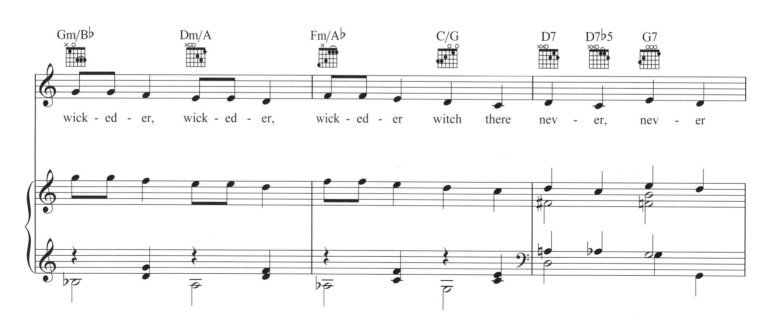

wick-ed-er, wick-ed-er, wick-ed-er witch there nev-er, nev-er

© 1938 (Renewed) METRO-GOLDWYN-MAYER INC.
© 1939 (Renewed) EMI FEIST CATALOG INC.
All Rights Administered by EMI FEIST CATALOG INC. (Publishing) and ALFRED MUSIC (Print)
All Rights Reserved   Used by Permission

EDELWEISS
from THE SOUND OF MUSIC

Lyrics by OSCAR HAMMERSTEIN II
Music by RICHARD RODGERS

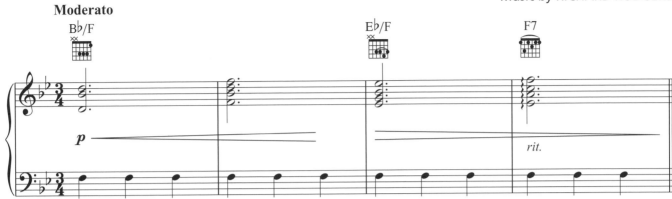

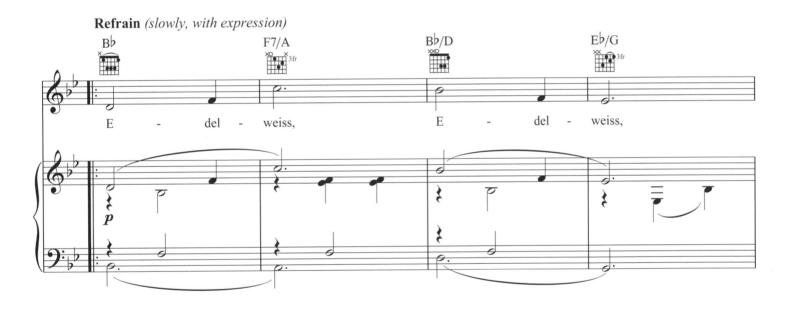

E - del - weiss, E - del - weiss,

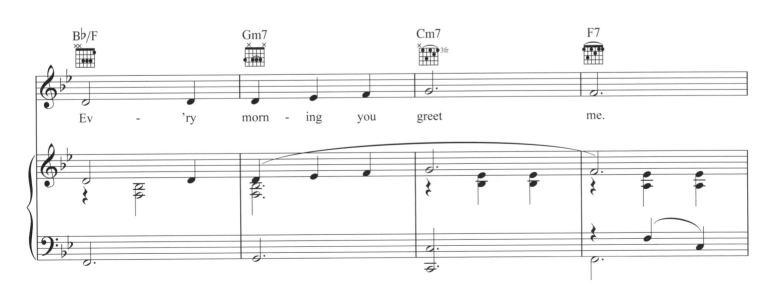

Ev - 'ry morn - ing you greet me.

Copyright © 1959 by Richard Rodgers and Oscar Hammerstein II
Copyright Renewed
Williamson Music, a Division of Rodgers & Hammerstein: an Imagem Company, owner of publication and allied rights throughout the world
International Copyright Secured   All Rights Reserved

EASTER PARADE
featured in the Motion Picture Irving Berlin's EASTER PARADE

Words and Music by
IRVING BERLIN

© Copyright 1933 by Irving Berlin
Copyright Renewed
International Copyright Secured   All Rights Reserved

FOR HE'S A JOLLY GOOD FELLOW

Traditional

Copyright © 2000 by HAL LEONARD CORPORATION
International Copyright Secured   All Rights Reserved

GHOSTBUSTERS
from the Columbia Motion Picture GHOSTBUSTERS

Words and Music by
RAY PARKER, JR.

* *Recorded a half step higher.*

© 1984 EMI GOLDEN TORCH MUSIC CORP. and RAYDIOLA MUSIC
Exclusive Print Rights for EMI GOLDEN TORCH MUSIC CORP. Administered by ALFRED MUSIC
All Rights Reserved   Used by Permission

Additional Lyrics

2. Who you gon' call? *(Ghostbusters!)*
   Mm, if you have a dose of a freaky ghost, baby, you'd better call *(Ghostbusters!)*

3. Don't get caught alone, oh no. *(Ghostbusters!)*
   When it comes through your door,
   Unless you just want some more, I think you better call *(Ghostbusters!)*

GO, TELL IT ON THE MOUNTAIN

African-American Spiritual
Verses by JOHN W. WORK, JR.

Moderate Swing

Go, tell it on the moun - tain,

O - ver the hills and ev - 'ry - where. Go, tell it on the

moun - tain, That Je - sus Christ is born.

While
The
Down

Copyright © 1991 by HAL LEONARD CORPORATION
International Copyright Secured   All Rights Reserved

GOD BLESS AMERICA

Words and Music by
IRVING BERLIN

© Copyright 1938, 1939 by Irving Berlin
Copyright Renewed 1965, 1966 by Irving Berlin
Copyright Assigned to the Trustees of the God Bless America Fund
International Copyright Secured   All Rights Reserved

GOOD NIGHT

Words and Music by JOHN LENNON
and PAUL McCARTNEY

Copyright © 1968 Sony/ATV Music Publishing LLC
Copyright Renewed
All Rights Administered by Sony/ATV Music Publishing LLC, 424 Church Street, Suite 1200, Nashville, TN 37219
International Copyright Secured   All Rights Reserved

GRANDFATHER'S CLOCK

By HENRY CLAY WORK

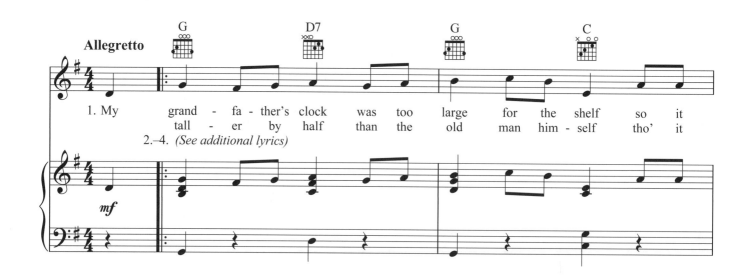

1. My grand-fa-ther's clock was too large for the shelf so it
   tall - er by half than the old man him-self tho' it
2.–4. *(See additional lyrics)*

stood nine-ty years on the floor. It was
weighed not a pen-ny-weight more. It was bought on the morn of the

day that he was born and was al - ways his treas - ure and pride. But it stopped short

Copyright © 2000 by HAL LEONARD CORPORATION
International Copyright Secured   All Rights Reserved

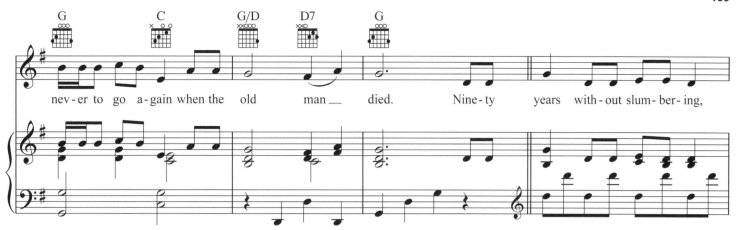

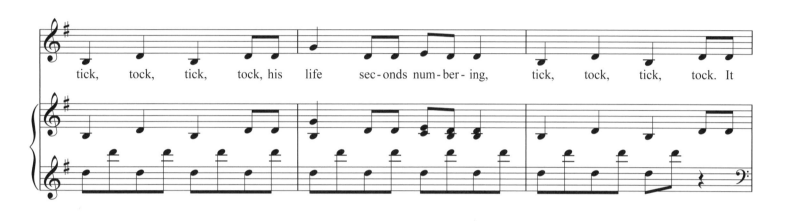

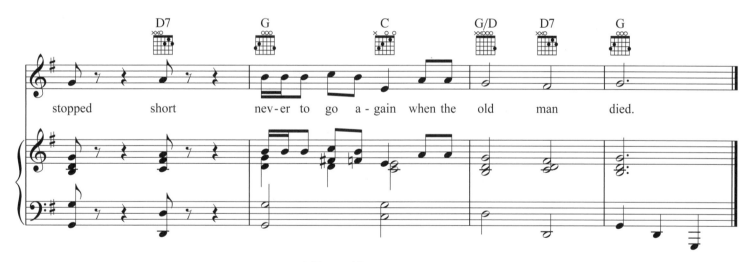

Additional Lyrics

2. In watching its pendulum swing to and fro,
   Many hours had he spent while a boy;
   And in childhood and manhood the clock seemed to know,
   And to share both his grief and his joy.
   For it struck twenty-four when he entered at the door,
   With a blooming and beautiful bride.
   Chorus

3. My grandfather said that of those he could hire,
   Not a servant so faithful he found;
   For it wasted no time, and had but one desire,
   At the close of each week to be wound.
   And it kept in its place, not a frown upon its face,
   And its hands never hung by its side.
   Chorus

4. It rang an alarm in the dead of the night,
   An alarm that for years had been dumb;
   And we knew that his spirit was pluming its flight,
   That his hour of departure had come.
   Still the clock kept the time, with a soft and muffled chime,
   As we silently stood by his side.
   Chorus

HAPPY BIRTHDAY TO YOU

Words and Music by MILDRED J. HILL
and PATTY S. HILL

© 1935 (Renewed) SUMMY-BIRCHARD MUSIC, a Division of SUMMY-BIRCHARD INC.
All Rights Administered by WB MUSIC CORP.
All Rights for Europe Controlled and Administered by KEITH PROWSE MUSIC CO.
All Rights Reserved   Used by Permission

HAPPY TRAILS

from the Television Series THE ROY ROGERS SHOW

Words and Music by
DALE EVANS

Copyright © 1952 Roy Rogers Music
Copyright Renewed
All Rights Administered by Sony/ATV Music Publishing LLC, 424 Church Street, Suite 1200, Nashville, TN 37219
International Copyright Secured   All Rights Reserved

HEART AND SOUL
from the Paramount Short Subject A SONG IS BORN

Words by FRANK LOESSER
Music by HOAGY CARMICHAEL

Copyright © 1938 Sony/ATV Music Publishing LLC
Copyright Renewed
All Rights Administered by Sony/ATV Music Publishing LLC, 424 Church Street, Suite 1200, Nashville, TN 37219
International Copyright Secured   All Rights Reserved

Moderately, lightly rhythmical

HI-LILI, HI-LO

Words by HELEN DEUTSCH
Music by BRONISLAU KAPER

A song of love is a sad song, hi-li-li, hi-li-li, hi-

lo. ___ A song of love is a song of woe, don't ask me

how I know. ___ A song of love is a sad

© 1952 (Renewed) METRO-GOLDWYN-MAYER INC.
All Rights Administered by EMI ROBBINS CATALOG INC. (Publishing) and ALFRED MUSIC (Print)
All Rights Reserved Used by Permission

THE HOKEY POKEY

Words and Music by CHARLES P. MACAK,
TAFFT BAKER and LARRY LaPRISE

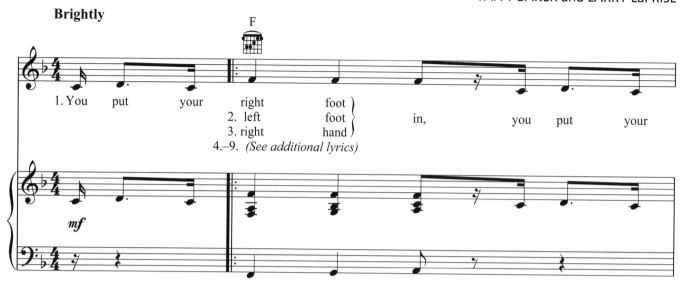

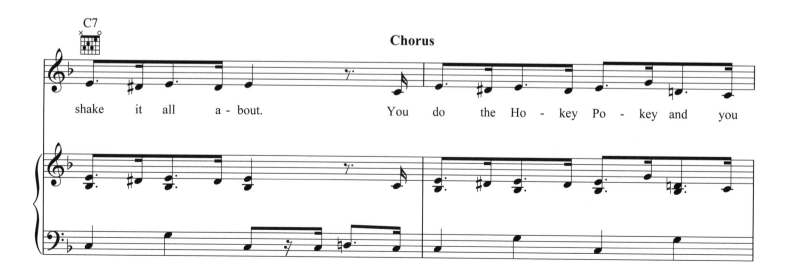

Copyright © 1950 Sony/ATV Music Publishing LLC
Copyright Renewed
All Rights Administered by Sony/ATV Music Publishing LLC, 424 Church Street, Suite 1200, Nashville, TN 37219
International Copyright Secured   All Rights Reserved

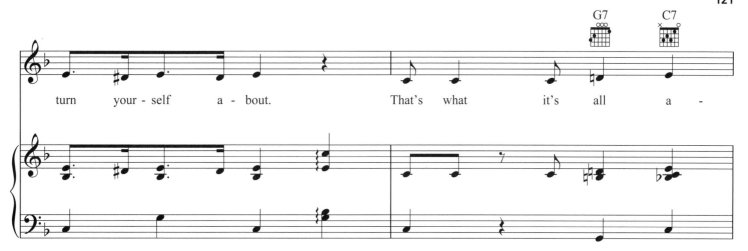

turn your-self a - bout. That's what it's all a -

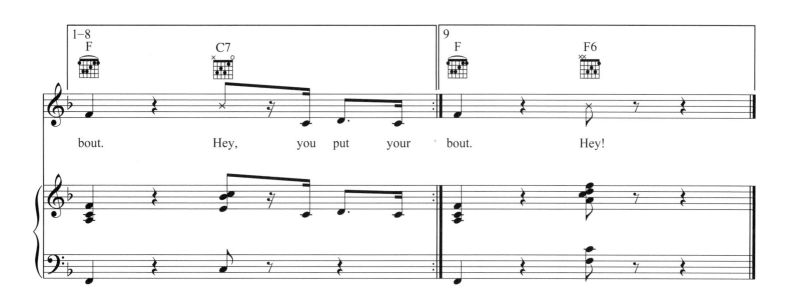

bout. Hey, you put your bout. Hey!

Additional Lyrics

4. Hey, you put your left hand in,
   You put your left hand out.
   You put your left hand in,
   And you shake it all about.
   Chorus

5. Hey, you put your right shoulder in,
   You put your right shoulder out.
   You put your right shoulder in,
   And you shake it all about.
   Chorus

6. Hey, you put your left shoulder in,
   You put your left shoulder out.
   You put your left shoulder in,
   And you shake it all about.
   Chorus

7. Hey, you put your right hip in,
   You put your right hip out.
   You put your right hip in,
   And you shake it all about.
   Chorus

8. Hey, you put your left hip in,
   You put your left hip out.
   You put your left hip in,
   And you shake it all about.
   Chorus

9. Hey, you put your whole self in,
   You put your whole self out.
   You put your whole self in,
   And you shake it all about.
   Chorus

HUSH, LITTLE BABY

Carolina Folk Lullaby

Copyright © 2000 by HAL LEONARD CORPORATION
International Copyright Secured All Rights Reserved

I'M AN OLD COWHAND
(From the Rio Grande)

Words and Music by
JOHNNY MERCER

© 1936 (Renewed) THE JOHNNY MERCER FOUNDATION
All Rights Administered by WB MUSIC CORP.
All Rights Reserved   Used by Permission

I WON'T GROW UP

from PETER PAN

Lyric by CAROLYN LEIGH
Music by MARK CHARLAP

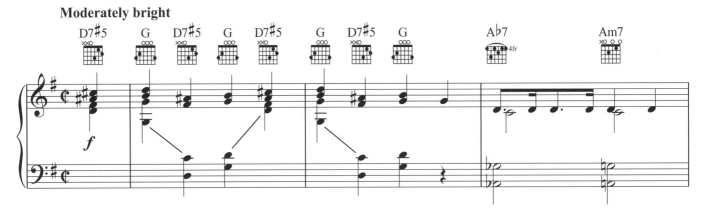

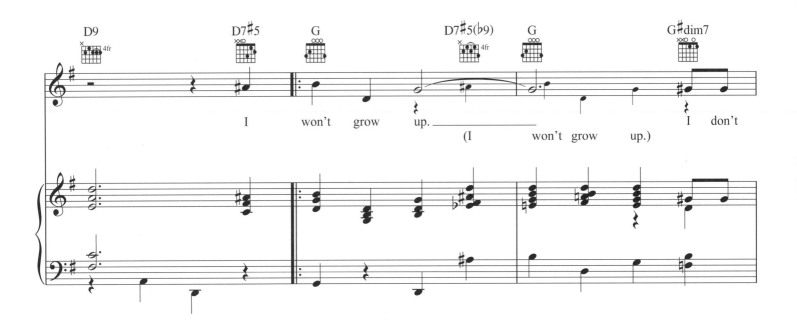

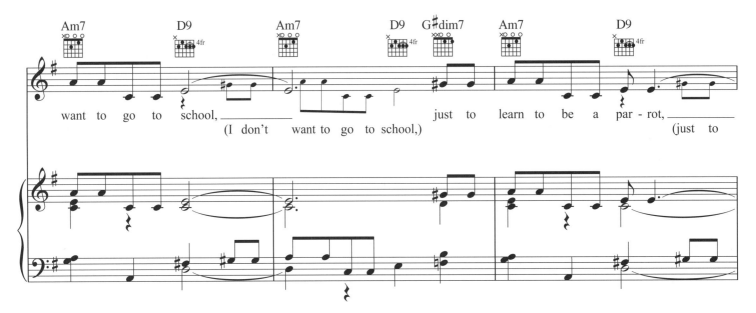

© 1954 (Renewed 1982) CAROLYN LEIGH and MARK CHARLAP
All Rights Controlled by EDWIN H. MORRIS & COMPANY, A Division of MPL Music Publishing, Inc. and CARWIN MUSIC INC.
All Rights Reserved

IF I ONLY HAD A BRAIN

from THE WIZARD OF OZ

Lyric by E.Y. "YIP" HARBURG
Music by HAROLD ARLEN

Scarecrow: Said a scare-crow swing-in' on a pole ___ to a black-bird sit-tin' on a
Tin Woodman: Said a tin-man rat-tlin' his ___ gibs ___ to a straw-man sad and wea-ry-
Cowardly Lion: Said a li-on, poor neu-rot-ic lion, ___ to a miss who lis-tened to him

fence, ___ "Oh! the Lord gave me a soul, ___ but for-
eyed, ___ "Oh! the Lord gave me tin ribs, ___ but for-
rave, ___ "Oh! the Lord made me a li-on, but the

© 1938 (Renewed) METRO-GOLDWYN-MAYER INC.
© 1939 (Renewed) EMI FEIST CATALOG INC.
All Rights Administered by EMI FEIST CATALOG INC. (Publishing) and ALFRED MUSIC (Print)
All Rights Reserved   Used by Permission

got to give me com - mon sense.___ If I had an ounce of com - mon
got to put a heart in - side."___ Then he banged his hol - low chest and
Lord for - got to make me brave."___ Then his tail be - gan to curl and

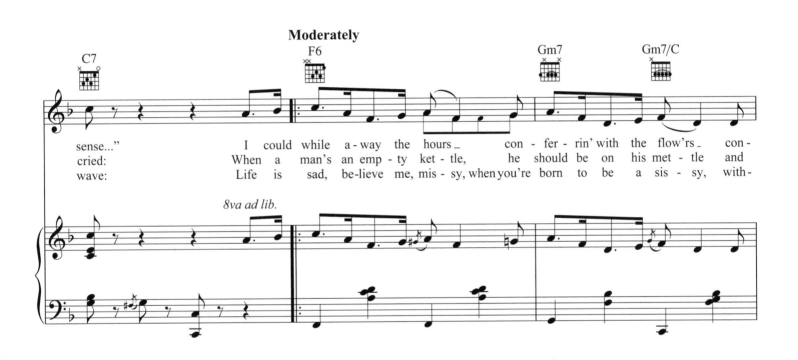

Moderately

sense..." I could while a - way the hours___ con - fer - rin' with the flow'rs___ con -
cried: When a man's an emp - ty ket - tle, he should be on his met - tle and
wave: Life is sad, be - lieve me, mis - sy, when you're born to be a sis - sy, with-

8va ad lib.

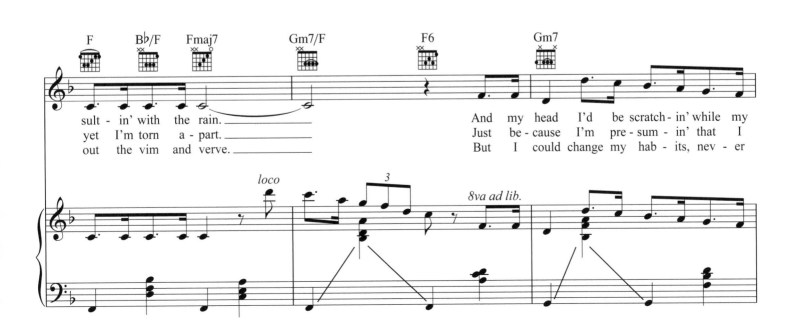

sult - in' with the rain. ___ And my head I'd be scratch - in' while my
yet I'm torn a - part. ___ Just be - cause I'm pre - sum - in' that I
out the vim and verve. ___ But I could change my hab - its, nev - er

loco   *3*   *8va ad lib.*

KUM BA YAH

Traditional Spiritual

Copyright © 1983 by HAL LEONARD CORPORATION
International Copyright Secured   All Rights Reserved

IF YOU'RE HAPPY AND YOU KNOW IT

Words and Music by
L. SMITH

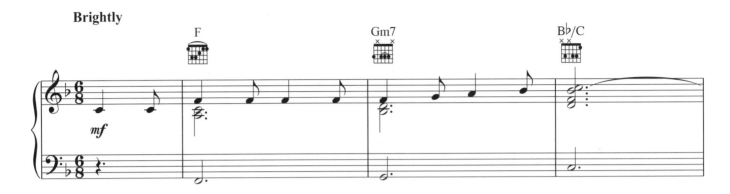

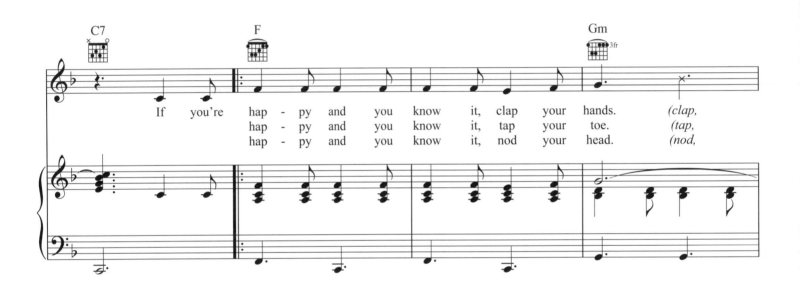

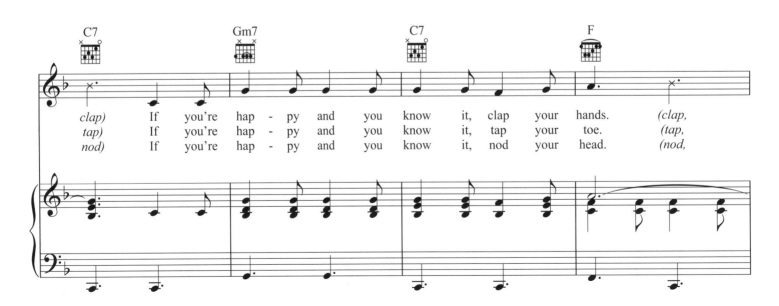

Copyright © 2000 by HAL LEONARD CORPORATION
International Copyright Secured   All Rights Reserved

LINUS AND LUCY

By VINCE GUARALDI

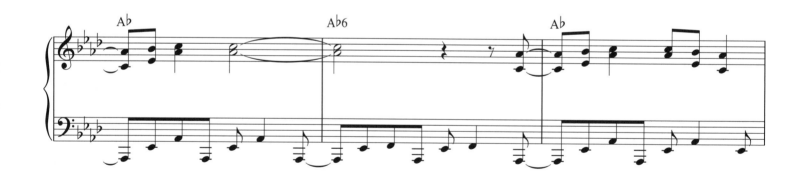

Copyright © 1965 LEE MENDELSON FILM PRODUCTIONS, INC.
Copyright Renewed
International Copyright Secured   All Rights Reserved

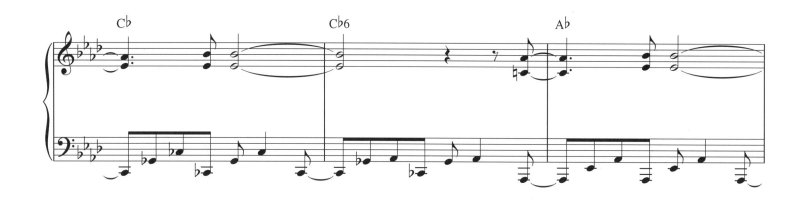

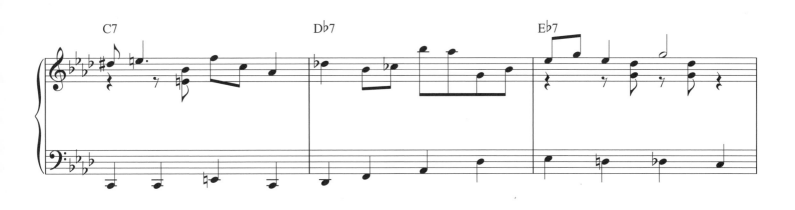

Original Tempo (♪♪ = ♪♪)

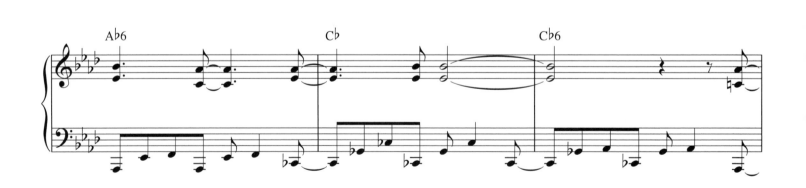

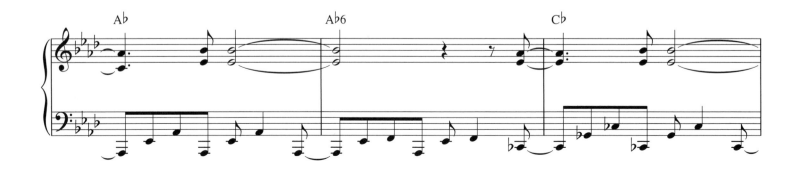

145

MARINE'S HYMN

Words by HENRY C. DAVIS
Melody based on a theme by JACQUES OFFENBACH

Copyright © 1991 by HAL LEONARD CORPORATION
International Copyright Secured   All Rights Reserved

ODE TO JOY

Words by HENRY VAN DYKE
Music by LUDWIG VAN BEETHOVEN

Copyright © 1994 by HAL LEONARD CORPORATION
International Copyright Secured   All Rights Reserved

MICKEY MOUSE MARCH

from Walt Disney's THE MICKEY MOUSE CLUB

Words and Music by
JIMMIE DODD

© 1955 Walt Disney Music Company
Copyright Renewed
All Rights Reserved   Used by Permission

MY COUNTRY, 'TIS OF THEE
(America)

Words by SAMUEL FRANCIS SMITH
Music from *Thesaurus Musicus*

Copyright © 1991 by HAL LEONARD CORPORATION
International Copyright Secured   All Rights Reserved

Additional Lyrics

3. Let music swell the breeze
   And ring from all the trees
   Sweet freedom's song.
   Let mortal tongues awake,
   Let all that breathe partake.
   Let rocks their silence break,
   The sound prolong.

4. Our father's God, to Thee,
   Author of liberty,
   To Thee we sing.
   Long may our land be bright
   With freedom's holy light.
   Protect us by Thy might,
   Great God, our King!

OVER THE RAINBOW
from THE WIZARD OF OZ

Music by HAROLD ARLEN
Lyric by E.Y. "YIP" HARBURG

© 1938 (Renewed) METRO-GOLDWYN-MAYER INC.
© 1939 (Renewed) EMI FEIST CATALOG INC.
All Rights Administered by EMI FEIST CATALOG INC. (Publishing) and ALFRED MUSIC (Print)
All Rights Reserved   Used by Permission

PETER COTTONTAIL

Words and Music by STEVE NELSON
and JACK ROLLINS

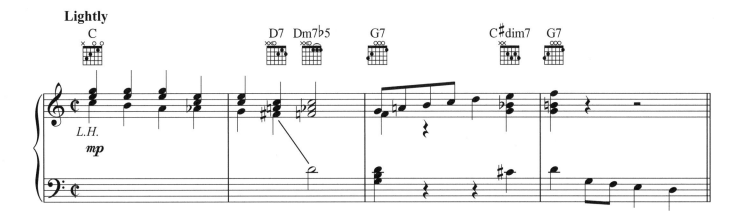

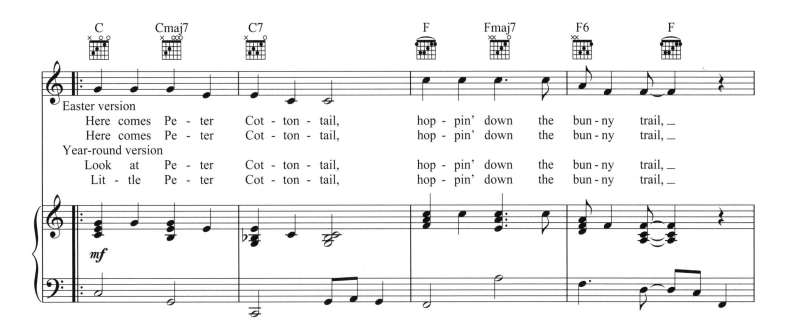

Easter version
Here comes Pe - ter Cot - ton - tail, hop - pin' down the bun - ny trail, __
Here comes Pe - ter Cot - ton - tail, hop - pin' down the bun - ny trail, __
Year-round version
Look at Pe - ter Cot - ton - tail, hop - pin' down the bun - ny trail, __
Lit - tle Pe - ter Cot - ton - tail, hop - pin' down the bun - ny trail, __

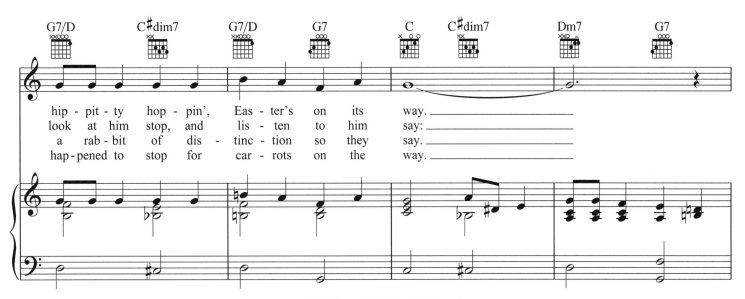

hip - pit - ty hop - pin', Eas - ter's on its way. _____
look at him stop, and lis - ten to him say:
a rab - bit of dis - tinc - tion so they say.
hap - pened to stop for car - rots on the way. _____

© 1950 (Renewed) CHAPPELL & CO., INC.
All Rights Reserved Used by Permission

PUFF THE MAGIC DRAGON

Words and Music by LENNY LIPTON
and PETER YARROW

*3rd time, play verse twice
before proceeding to Chorus

Copyright © 1963; Renewed 1991 Honalee Melodies (ASCAP) and Silver Dawn Music (ASCAP)
Worldwide Rights for Honalee Melodies Administered by BMG Rights Management (US) LLC
Worldwide Rights for Silver Dawn Music Administered by WB Music Corp.
International Copyright Secured   All Rights Reserved

Additional Lyrics

2. Together they would travel on a boat with billowed sail.
   Jackie kept a lookout perched on Puff's gigantic tail.
   Noble kings and princes would bow whene'er they came.
   Pirate ships would low'r their flags when Puff roared out his name. Oh!
   Chorus

3. A dragon lives forever, but not so little boys.
   Painted wings and giant rings make way for other toys.
   One gray night it happened, Jackie Paper came no more,
   And Puff that mighty dragon, he ceased his fearless roar.

4. His head was bent in sorrow, green tears fell like rain.
   Puff no longer went to play along the Cherry Lane.
   Without his lifelong friend, Puff could not be brave,
   So Puff that mighty dragon sadly slipped into his cave. Oh!
   Chorus

THE RETURN OF PUFF

5. Puff the magic dragon danced down the Cherry Lane.
   He came upon a little girl, Julie Maple was her name.
   She'd heard that Puff had gone away, but that can never be,
   So together they went sailing to the land called Honalee.
   Chorus

PUT ON A HAPPY FACE

from BYE BYE BIRDIE

Lyric by LEE ADAMS
Music by CHARLES STROUSE

© 1960 (Renewed) STRADA MUSIC
All Rights Administered by WB MUSIC CORP.
All Rights Reserved   Used by Permission

SKATING
from A CHARLIE BROWN CHRISTMAS

By VINCE GUARALDI

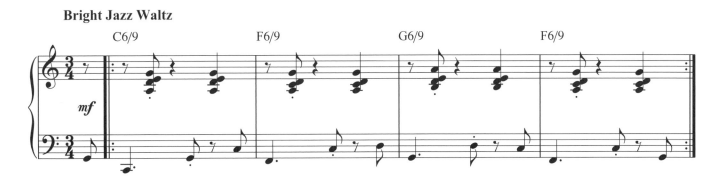

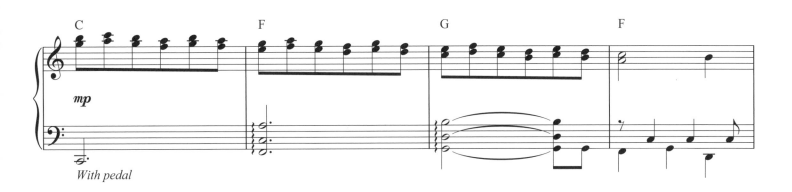

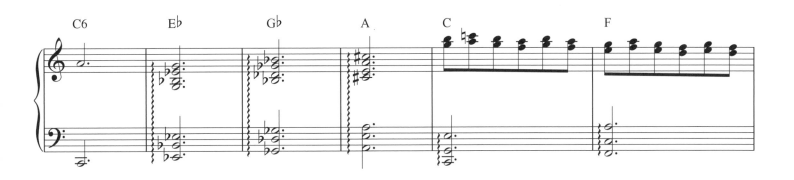

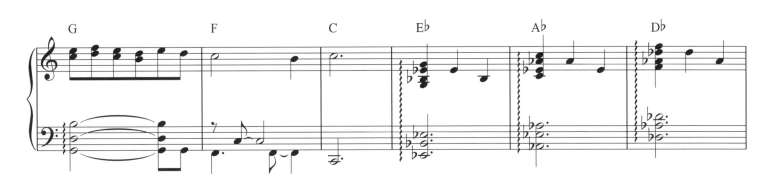

Copyright © 1966 LEE MENDELSON FILM PRODUCTIONS, INC.
Copyright Renewed
International Copyright Secured   All Rights Reserved

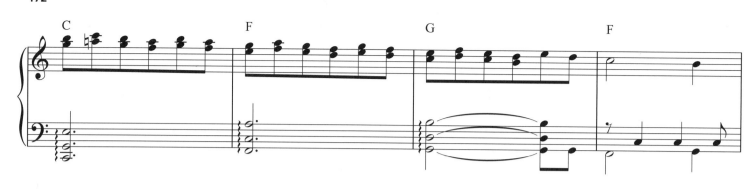

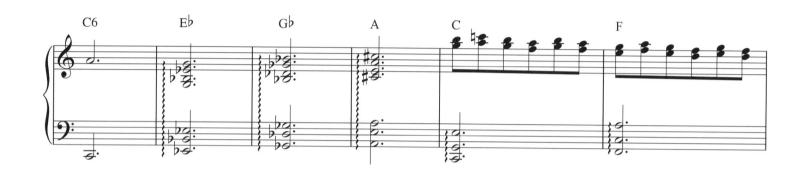

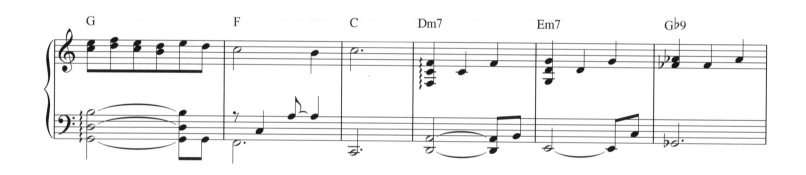

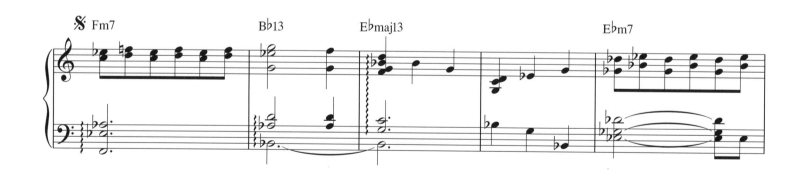

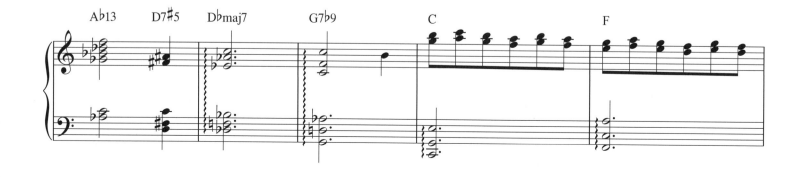

THE RIVER SEINE
(La Seine)

Words by ALLAN ROBERTS and ALAN HOLT
Original French Text by FLAVIEN MONOD and GUY LaFARGE

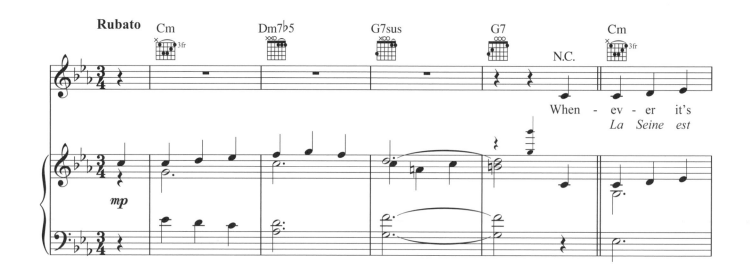

When- ev- er it's
La Seine est

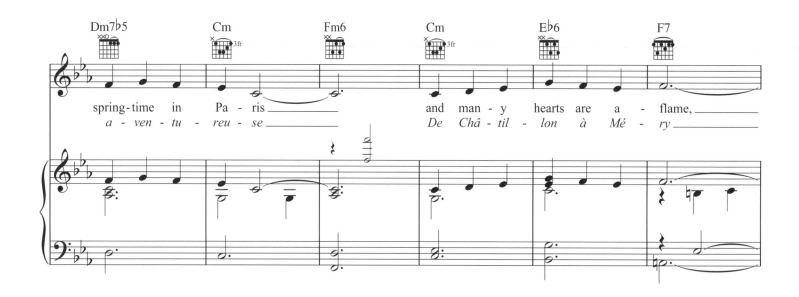

spring- time in Pa- ris _____ and man- y hearts are a- flame, _____
a- ven- tu- reu- se _____ De Châ- til- lon à Mé- ry _____

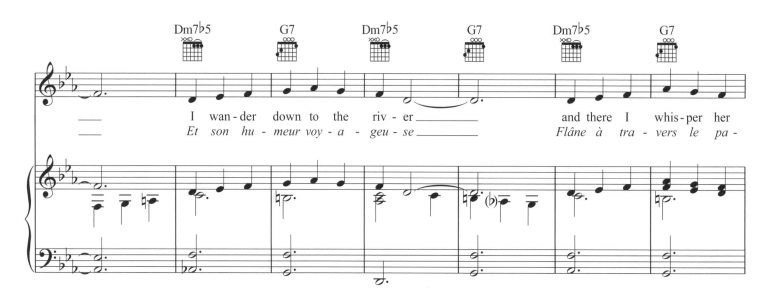

I wan- der down to the riv- er _____ and there I whis- per her
Et son hu- meur voy- a- geu- se _____ Flâne à tra- vers le pa-

© 1953 (Renewed) WB MUSIC CORP. and MUSIC SALES CORPORATION
All Rights Reserved Used by Permission

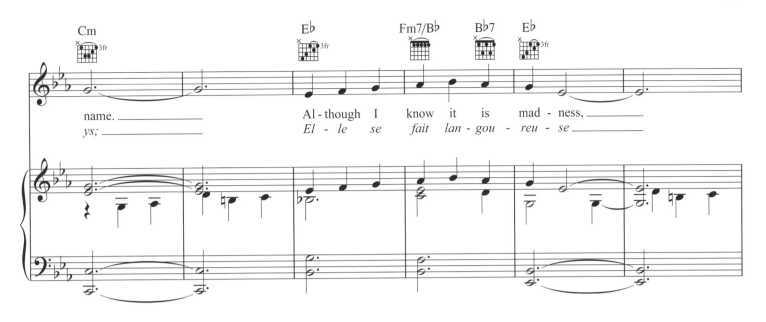

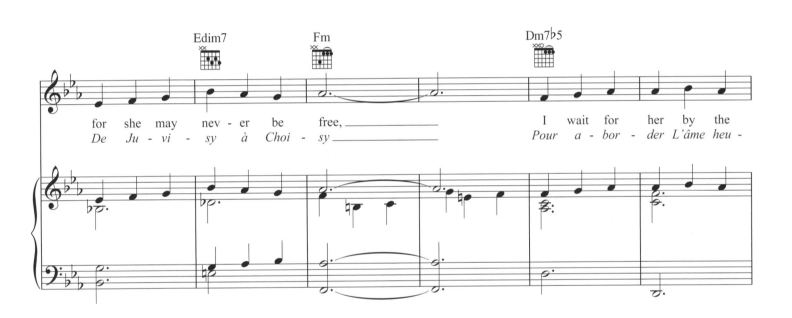

Moderate Waltz

SCARBOROUGH FAIR

Traditional English

Moderately and freely

1. Are you go-ing to Scar-bor-ough Fair?
2. Have (him) (her) make me a cam-bric shirt,
3. Have (him) (her) wash it in yon-der dry well,

4.–6. *(See additional lyrics)*

Pars - ley, sage, _____ rose - mar - y and
pars - ley, sage, _____ rose - mar - y and
pars - ley, sage, _____ rose - mar - y and

Copyright © 2009 by HAL LEONARD CORPORATION
International Copyright Secured   All Rights Reserved

Additional Lyrics

4. Have him (her) find me an acre of land,
   Parsley, sage, rosemary and thyme.
   Between the sea and over the sand,
   And then he'll (she'll) be a true love of mine.

5. Plow the land with the horn of a lamb,
   Parsley, sage, rosemary and thyme.
   Then sow some seeds from north of the dam,
   And then he'll (she'll) be a true love of mine.

6. If he (she) tells me he (she) can't I'll reply:
   Parsley, sage, rosemary and thyme.
   Let me know that at least he (she) will try,
   And then he'll (she'll) be a true love of mine.

SIMPLE GIFTS

Traditional Shaker Hymn

'Tis the gift to be sim-ple, 'tis the gift to be free, 'tis the gift to come down where we ought to be, and when we find our-selves in the

Copyright © 1996 by HAL LEONARD CORPORATION
International Copyright Secured   All Rights Reserved

THEME FROM THE SIMPSONS™

from THE SIMPSONS

Music by DANNY ELFMAN

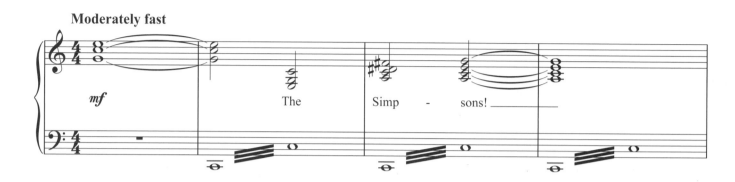

Copyright © 1990, 1991 Fox Film Music Corporation
All Rights Reserved   Used by Permission
The Simpsons TM & © 1990 Twentieth Century Fox Film Corporation

SING

from SESAME STREET

Words and Music by
JOE RAPOSO

Moderately

mp

With pedal

Sing! Sing a song.

Sing out loud, sing out strong.

Sing of good things, not bad;

Copyright © 1971 by Jonico Music, Inc.
Copyright Renewed
All Rights in the U.S.A. Administered by Green Fox Music, Inc.
International Copyright Secured All Rights Reserved

SO LONG, FAREWELL

from THE SOUND OF MUSIC

Lyrics by OSCAR HAMMERSTEIN II
Music by RICHARD RODGERS

Copyright © 1959, 1960 by Richard Rodgers and Oscar Hammerstein II
Copyright Renewed
Williamson Music, a Division of Rodgers & Hammerstein: an Imagem Company, owner of publication and allied rights throughout the world
International Copyright Secured   All Rights Reserved

hate to go and miss this pret - ty sight. _

So long, fare - well, Auf wie - der - sehn, a - dieu, _ a -

dieu, A - dieu, to yieu and yieu and yieu. _

THE SOUND OF MUSIC
from THE SOUND OF MUSIC

Lyrics by OSCAR HAMMERSTEIN II
Music by RICHARD RODGERS

Molto moderato *(tenderly)*

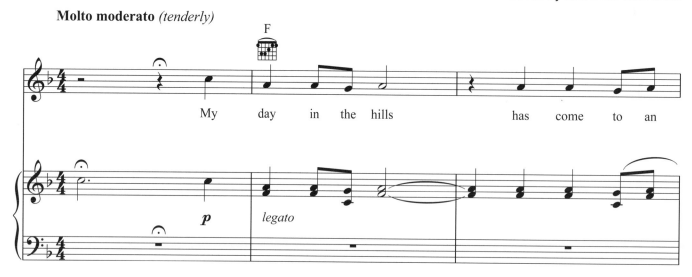

Copyright © 1959 by Richard Rodgers and Oscar Hammerstein II
Copyright Renewed
Williamson Music, a Division of Rodgers & Hammerstein: an Imagem Company, owner of publication and allied rights throughout the world
International Copyright Secured   All Rights Reserved

SPLISH SPLASH

Words and Music by BOBBY DARIN
and MURRAY KAUFMAN

Copyright © 1958 by Unart Music Corporation
Copyright Renewed and Assigned to Alley Music Corp., Trio Music Company and EMI Unart Catalog Inc.
All Rights for Alley Music Corp. and Trio Music Company Administered by Hudson Bay Music Inc.
All Rights for EMI Unart Catalog Inc. Administered by Hudson Bay Music Inc. (Publishing) and Alfred Music (Print)
International Copyright Secured   All Rights Reserved
Used by Permission

SPONGEBOB SQUAREPANTS THEME SONG

from SPONGEBOB SQUAREPANTS

Words and Music by MARK HARRISON,
BLAISE SMITH, STEVE HILLENBURG
and DEREK DRYMON

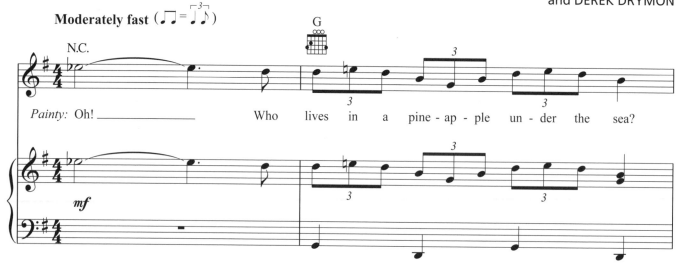

Painty: Oh! _____ Who lives in a pine-ap-ple un-der the sea?

Kids: Sponge - Bob Square - Pants! *Painty:* Ab - sor-bent and yel-low and por-ous is he.

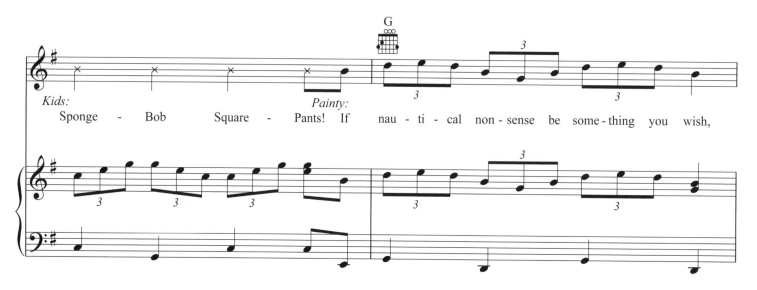

Kids: Sponge - Bob Square - Pants! *Painty:* If nau-ti-cal non-sense be some-thing you wish,

Copyright © 2001 Tunes By Nickelodeon, Inc.
All Rights Administered by Sony/ATV Music Publishing LLC, 424 Church Street, Suite 1200, Nashville, TN 37219
International Copyright Secured   All Rights Reserved

THE STAR-SPANGLED BANNER

Words by FRANCIS SCOTT KEY
Music by JOHN STAFFORD SMITH

Copyright © 1995 by HAL LEONARD CORPORATION
International Copyright Secured   All Rights Reserved

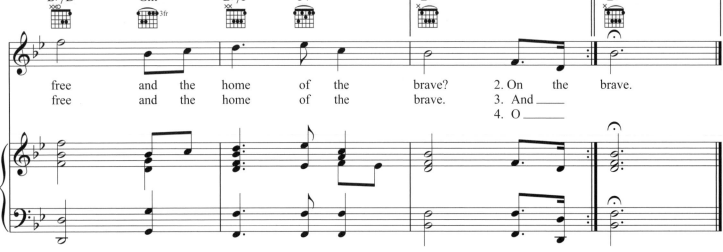

Additional Lyrics

3. And where is the band who so vauntingly swore,
   'Mid the havoc of war and the battle's confusion,
   A home and a country they'd leave us no more?
   Their blood has wash'd out their foul footstep's pollution.
   No refuge could save the hireling and slave
   From the terror of flight or the gloom of the grave.
   And the star-spangled banner in triumph doth wave
   O'er the land of the free and the home of the brave.

4. O thus be it ever when free men shall stand,
   Between their loved homes and the war's desolation.
   Blest with vict'ry and peace, may the heav'n rescued land
   Praise the Power that hath made and preserved us a nation!
   Then conquer we must when our cause it is just,
   And this be our motto, "In God is our trust!"
   And the star-spangled banner in triumph shall wave
   O'er the land of the free and the home of the brave.

TAKE ME OUT TO THE BALL GAME

Words by JACK NORWORTH
Music by ALBERT VON TILZER

Spirited, in 1

Copyright © 1994 HAL LEONARD CORPORATION
International Copyright Secured   All Rights Reserved

THE SYNCOPATED CLOCK

Music by LEROY ANDERSON
Words by MITCHELL PARISH

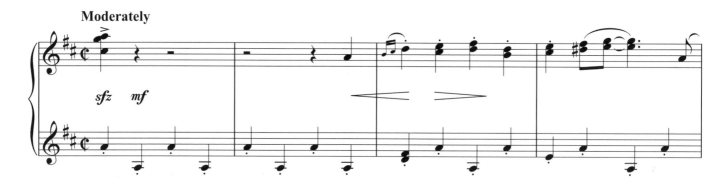

© 1946, 1951 (Copyrights Renewed) WOODBURY MUSIC COMPANY and EMI MILLS MUSIC INC.
All Rights for EMI MILLS MUSIC INC. Administered by EMI MILLS MUSIC INC. (Publishing) and ALFRED MUSIC (Print)
All Rights Reserved   Used by Permission

THIS IS MY COUNTRY

Words by DON RAYE
Music by AL JACOBS

© 1940 SHAWNEE PRESS, INC.
© Renewed SHAWNEE PRESS, INC. and WAROCK CORP.
All Rights Reserved

heart is filled with love for all of these. I
all I love is here with - in her gates. My

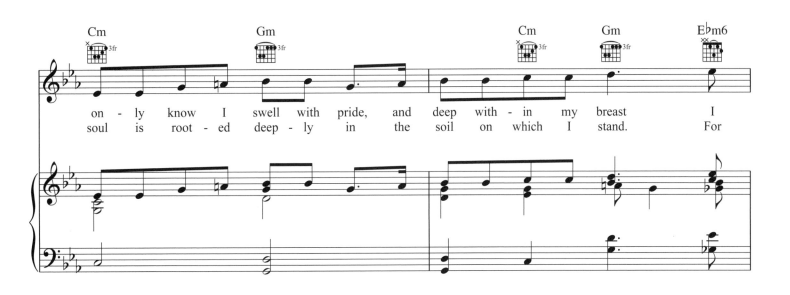

on - ly know I swell with pride, and deep with - in my breast I
soul is root - ed deep - ly in the soil on which I stand. For

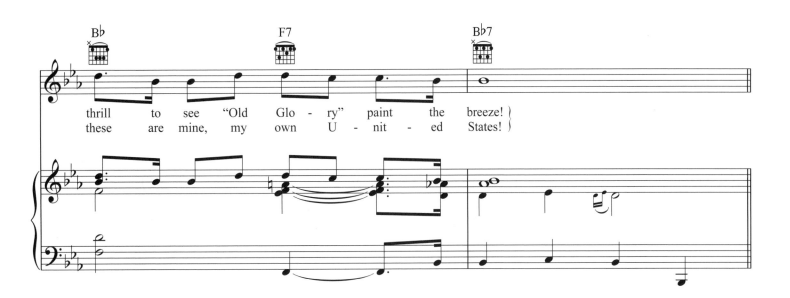

thrill to see "Old Glo - ry" paint the breeze!
these are mine, my own U - nit - ed States!

THIS LAND IS YOUR LAND

Words and Music by
WOODY GUTHRIE

Bright and cheerful

WGP/TRO - © Copyright 1956, 1958, 1970, 1972 (Copyrights Renewed) Woody Guthrie Publications, Inc. and Ludlow Music, Inc., New York, NY
All Rights Administered by Ludlow Music, Inc.
International Copyright Secured
All Rights Reserved Including Public Performance For Profit
Used by Permission

low me _____ that gold - en val - ley; _____
for - est _____ to the Gulf Stream wa - ters; _____
round me _____ a voice was sound - ing; _____
lift - ing, _____ a voice was chant - ing: _____

this land was made for you and

me. _____
{ 2.,4.,6. This land is
3. I've roamed and _____ me. _____
5. Well, the sun came

rit.

TOMORROW
from the Musical Production ANNIE

Lyric by MARTIN CHARNIN
Music by CHARLES STROUSE

Moderately slow

The sun-'ll come out _____ to-mor-row, bet your bot-tom dol-lar that to-mor-row _____ there'll be sun! Jus' think-ing a-bout _____ to-mor-row

© 1977 (Renewed) EDWIN H. MORRIS & COMPANY, A Division of MPL Music Publishing, Inc. and CHARLES STROUSE PUBLISHING
All Rights for CHARLES STROUSE PUBLISHING Administered by WB MUSIC CORP.
All Rights Reserved   Used by Permission

UNDER THE SEA
from Walt Disney's THE LITTLE MERMAID

Music by ALAN MENKEN
Lyrics by HOWARD ASHMAN

The sea - weed is al - ways green - er
Down here ___ all the fish is hap - py

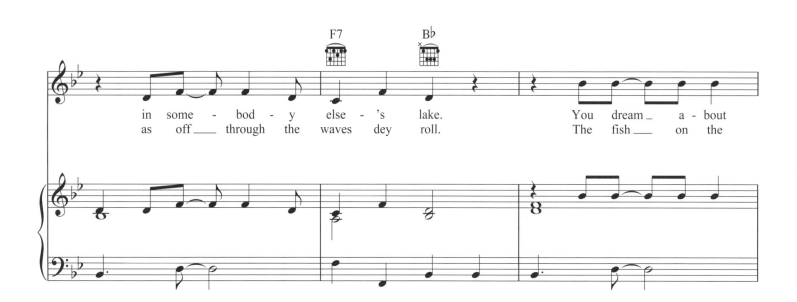

in some - bod - y else - 's lake.
as off ___ through the waves dey roll.

You dream ___ a - bout
The fish ___ on the

© 1988 Wonderland Music Company, Inc. and Walt Disney Music Company
All Rights Reserved   Used by Permission

oh,   that   blow - fish   blow.

Un - der the   sea.   Un - der the   sea.

When _ the sar - dine be - gin _ the   be - guine, it's   mu - sic to

THE UNICORN

Words and Music by
SHEL SILVERSTEIN

long time a-go when the earth was green, — there was more kinds of an-i-mals than
2.–6. *(See additional lyrics)*

you've ev-er seen. And they'd run a-round free while the world was be-ing born, and the

TRO - © Copyright 1962 (Renewed) and 1968 (Renewed) Hollis Music, Inc., New York, NY
International Copyright Secured
All Rights Reserved Including Public Performance For Profit
Used by Permission

Additional Lyrics

2. But the Lord seen some sinnin' and it caused him pain.
   He says, "Stand back, I'm gonna make it rain.
   So hey, Brother Noah, I'll tell you what to do.
   Go and build me a floating zoo."
   Chorus
   "And you take two alligators and a couple of geese,
   Two humpback camels and two chimpanzees,
   Two cats, two rats, two elephants. But, sure as you're born,
   Noah, don't you forget my unicorns."

3. Now Noah was there and he answered the callin'
   And he finished up the ark as the rain started fallin'.
   Then he marched in the animals two by two,
   And he sung out as they went through:
   Chorus
   "Hey Lord, I got you two alligators and a couple of geese,
   Two humpback camels and two chimpanzees,
   Two cats, two rats, two elephants. But, sure as you're born,
   Lord, I just don't see your unicorns."

4. Well, Noah looked out through the drivin' rain,
   But the unicorns was hidin' – playin' silly games.
   They were kickin' and a-splashin' while the rain was pourin'.
   Oh, them foolish unicorns.
   Chorus
   "And you take two alligators and a couple of geese,
   Two humpback camels and two chimpanzees,
   Two cats, two rats, two elephants. But, sure as you're born,
   Noah, don't you forget my unicorns."

5. Then the ducks started duckin' and the snakes started snakin',
   And the elephants started elephantin' and the boat started shakin'.
   The mice started squeakin' and the lions started roarin',
   And everyone's aboard but them unicorns.
   Chorus
   I mean the two alligators and a couple of geese,
   The humpback camels and the chimpanzees.
   Noah cried, "Close the door 'cause the rain is pourin',
   And we just can't wait for them unicorns."

6. And then the ark started movin' and it drifted with the tide,
   And the unicorns looked up from the rock and cried.
   And the water came up and sort of floated them away,
   That's why you've never seen a unicorn to this day.
   Chorus
   You'll see a lot of alligators and a whole mess of geese,
   You'll see humpback camels and chimpanzees,
   You'll see cats and rats and elephants. But, sure as you're born,
   You're never gonna see no unicorn.

WHERE IS LOVE?
from the Broadway Musical OLIVER!

Words and Music by
LIONEL BART

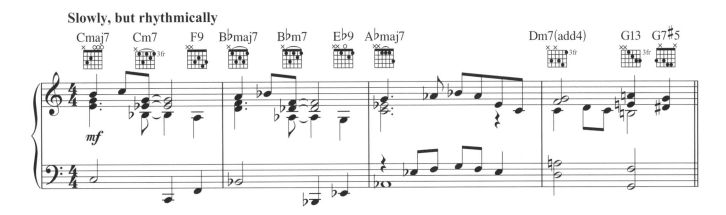

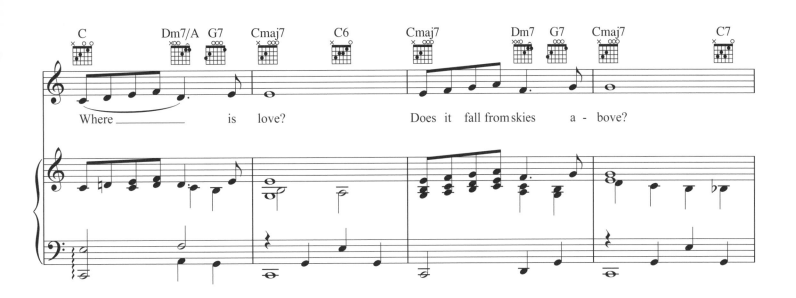

Where _____ is love? Does it fall from skies a-bove?

Is it un-der-neath the wil-low tree _ that I've been dream-ing of?

© Copyright 1960 (Renewed), 1968 (Renewed) Lakeview Music Co., Ltd., London, England
TRO - Hollis Music, Inc., New York, controls all publication rights for the U.S.A. and Canada
International Copyright Secured
All Rights Reserved Including Public Performance For Profit
Used by Permission

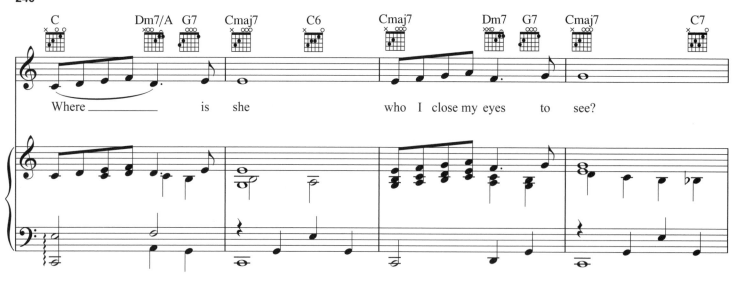

Where _____ is she who I close my eyes to see?

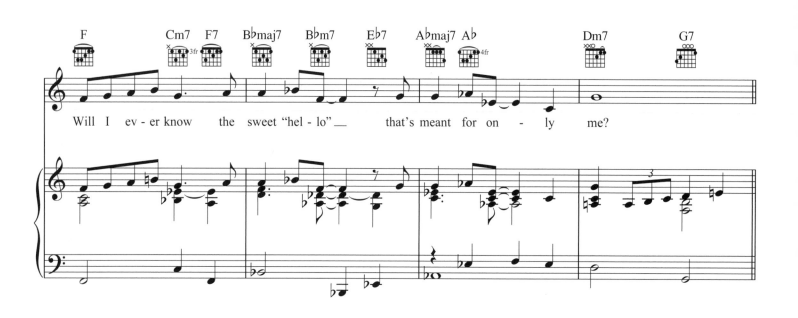

Will I ev - er know the sweet "hel - lo" __ that's meant for on - ly me?

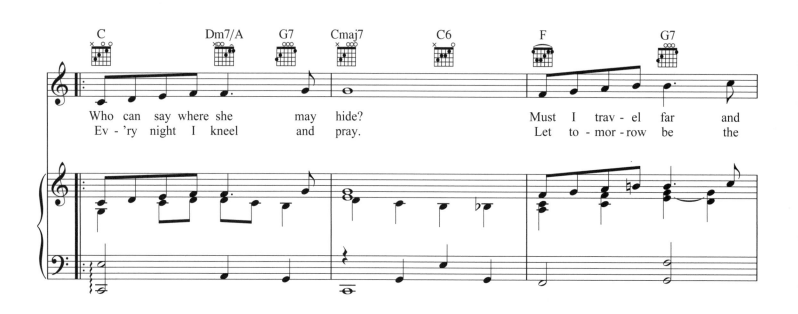

Who can say where she may hide?
Ev - 'ry night I kneel and pray.

Must I trav - el far and
Let to - mor - row be the

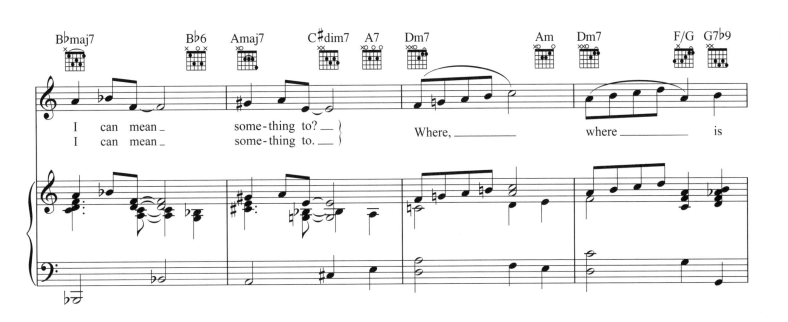

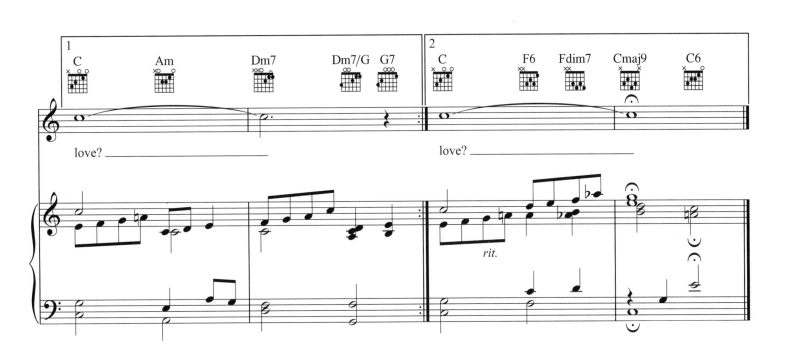

WE'RE OFF TO SEE THE WIZARD

from THE WIZARD OF OZ

Lyric by E.Y. "YIP" HARBURG
Music by HAROLD ARLEN

Moderately

Lyrics:

Fol - low the yel - low brick road, _____ fol - low the yel - low brick road, _____

fol - low, fol - low, fol - low, fol - low, fol - low the yel - low brick road. _____

© 1938 (Renewed) METRO-GOLDWYN-MAYER INC.
© 1939 (Renewed) EMI FEIST CATALOG INC.
All Rights Administered by EMI FEIST CATALOG INC. (Publishing) and ALFRED MUSIC (Print)
All Rights Reserved   Used by Permission

WHAT I LIKE ABOUT YOU

Words and Music by MICHAEL SKILL,
WALLY PALAMARCHUK and JAMES MARINOS

Bright Rock

Add bass on repeat

© 1979 EMI APRIL MUSIC INC.
All Rights Reserved   International Copyright Secured   Used by Permission

WHEN I GROW TOO OLD TO DREAM

Lyric by OSCAR HAMMERSTEIN II
Music by SIGMUND ROMBERG

Moderate Waltz

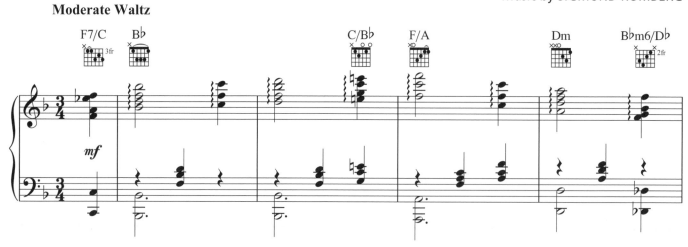

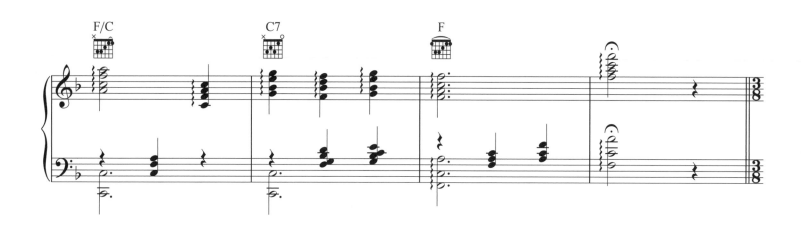

We have been gay go-ing our way. Life has been
Af-ter you've gone life will go on. Time will be

© 1934 (Renewed) EMI ROBBINS CATALOG INC.
All Rights Administered by EMI ROBBINS CATALOG INC. (Publishing) and ALFRED MUSIC (Print)
All Rights Reserved   Used by Permission

WHEN THE SAINTS GO MARCHING IN

Words by KATHERINE E. PURVIS
Music by JAMES M. BLACK

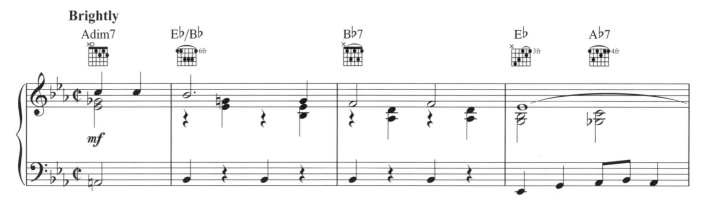

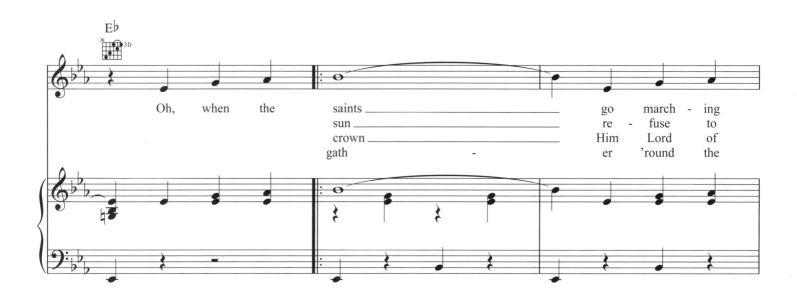

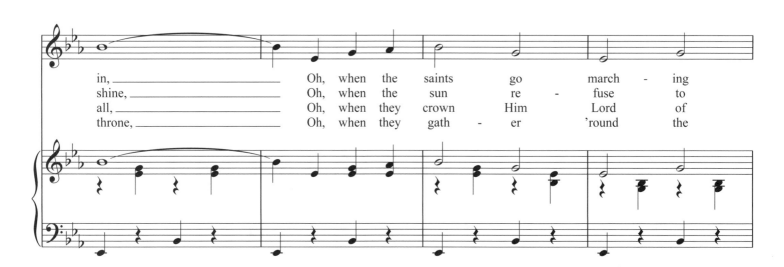

Copyright © 1994 by HAL LEONARD CORPORATION
International Copyright Secured   All Rights Reserved

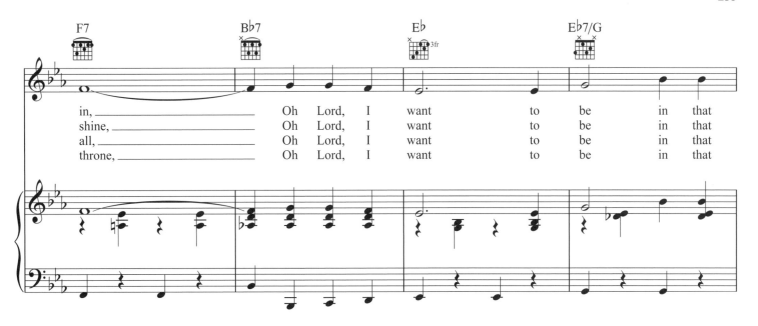

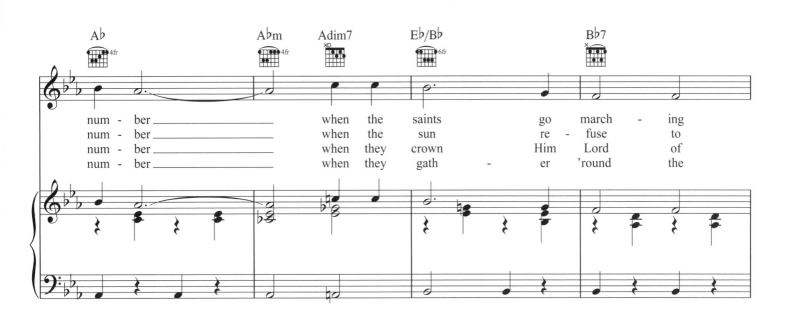

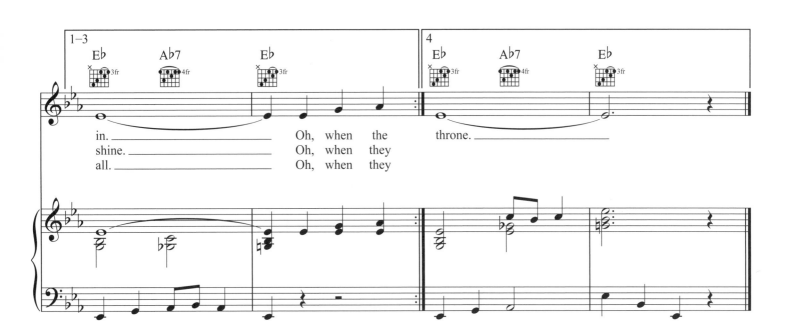

WON'T YOU BE MY NEIGHBOR?
(It's a Beautiful Day in the Neighborhood)
from MISTER ROGERS' NEIGHBORHOOD

Words and Music by
FRED ROGERS

Copyright © 1967 by Fred M. Rogers
Copyright Renewed
International Copyright Secured   All Rights Reserved

YOU'RE A GRAND OLD FLAG

Words and Music by
GEORGE M. COHAN

March tempo

Copyright © 1991 by HAL LEONARD CORPORATION
International Copyright Secured   All Rights Reserved

YOU'VE GOT A FRIEND IN ME

from Walt Disney's TOY STORY

Music and Lyrics by
RANDY NEWMAN

You've got a friend in me.___
You've got a friend in me.___

You've got a friend in me.__
You've got a friend in me.__

When the road__ looks rough a - head__ and you're miles__
You got trou - bles, then I got 'em, too.__

© 1995 Walt Disney Music Company
All Rights Reserved   Used by Permission

YOU ARE MY SUNSHINE

Words and Music by
JIMMIE DAVIS

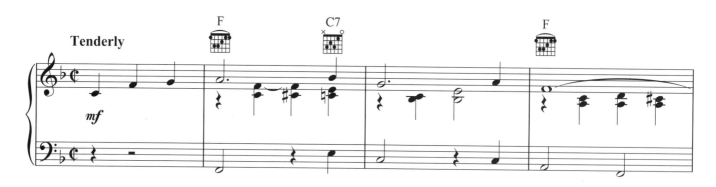

The oth - er night, dear, _____ as I lay
love you _____ and make you
once, dear, _____ you real - ly

sleep - ing _____ I dreamed I held you in my
hap - py _____ if you will on - ly say the
loved me _____ and no one else could come be -

Copyright © 1930 by Peer International Corporation
Copyright Renewed
International Copyright Secured   All Rights Reserved

THE BEST EVER
COLLECTION
ARRANGED FOR PIANO, VOICE AND GUITAR

100 of the Most Beautiful Piano Solos Ever
100 songs
00102787 ....$27.50

150 of the Most Beautiful Songs Ever
150 ballads
00360735 ....$27.00

150 More of the Most Beautiful Songs Ever
150 songs
00311318 ....$29.99

More of the Best Acoustic Rock Songs Ever
69 tunes
00311738 ....$19.95

Best Acoustic Rock Songs Ever
65 acoustic hits
00310984 ....$19.95

Best Big Band Songs Ever
68 big band hits
00359129 ....$17.99

Best Blues Songs Ever
73 blues tunes
00312874 ....$19.99

Best Broadway Songs Ever
83 songs
00309155 ....$24.99

More of the Best Broadway Songs Ever
82 songs
00311501 ....$22.95

Best Children's Songs Ever
102 songs
00310358 ....$22.99

Best Christmas Songs Ever
69 holiday favorites
00359130 ....$24.99

Best Classic Rock Songs Ever
64 hits
00310800 ....$22.99

Best Classical Music Ever
86 classical favorites
00310674 (Piano Solo) $19.95

The Best Country Rock Songs Ever
52 hits
00118881 ....$19.99

Best Country Songs Ever
78 classic country hits
00359135 ....$19.99

Best Disco Songs Ever
50 songs
00312565 ....$19.99

Best Dixieland Songs Ever
90 songs
00312326 ....$19.99

Best Early Rock 'n' Roll Songs Ever
74 songs
00310816 ....$19.95

Best Easy Listening Songs Ever
75 mellow favorites
00359193 ....$19.99

Best Folk/Pop Songs Ever
66 hits
00138299 ....$19.99

Best Gospel Songs Ever
80 gospel songs
00310503 ....$19.99

Best Hymns Ever
118 hymns
00310774 ....$18.99

Best Jazz Piano Solos Ever
80 songs
00312079 ....$19.99

Best Jazz Standards Ever
77 jazz hits
00311641 ....$19.95

More of the Best Jazz Standards Ever
74 beloved jazz hits
00311023 ....$19.95

Best Latin Songs Ever
67 songs
00310355 ....$19.99

Best Love Songs Ever
62 favorite love songs
00359198 ....$19.99

Best Movie Songs Ever
71 songs
00310063 ....$19.99

Best Pop/Rock Songs Ever
50 classics
00138279 ....$19.99

Best Praise & Worship Songs Ever
80 all-time favorites
00311057 ....$22.99

More of the Best Praise & Worship Songs Ever
76 songs
00311800 ....$24.99

Best R&B Songs Ever
66 songs
00310184 ....$19.95

Best Rock Songs Ever
63 songs
00490424 ....$18.95

Best Showtunes Ever
71 songs
00118782 ....$19.99

Best Songs Ever
72 must-own classics
00359224 ....$24.99

Best Soul Songs Ever
70 hits
00311427 ....$19.95

Best Standards Ever, Vol. 1 (A-L)
72 beautiful ballads
00359231 ....$17.95

Best Standards Ever, Vol. 2 (M-Z)
73 songs
00359232 ....$17.99

More of the Best Standards Ever, Vol. 1 (A-L)
76 all-time favorites
00310813 ....$17.95

More of the Best Standards Ever, Vol. 2 (M-Z)
75 stunning standards
00310814 ....$17.95

Best Torch Songs Ever
70 sad and sultry favorites
00311027 ....$19.95

Best Wedding Songs Ever
70 songs
00311096 ....$19.95

Prices, contents and availability subject to change without notice. Not all products available outside the U.S.A.

HAL•LEONARD®
CORPORATION
7777 W. BLUEMOUND RD. P.O. BOX 13819 MILWAUKEE, WI 53213

Visit us online for complete songlists at
www.halleonard.com

0615

THE **MOST REQUESTED** SERIES FROM

 cherry lane music company

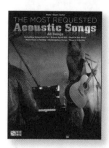      

THE MOST REQUESTED ACOUSTIC SONGS

American Pie • Better Together • Black Water • The Boxer • Cat's in the Cradle • Crazy Little Thing Called Love • Free Fallin' • Friend of the Devil • I Walk the Line • I've Just Seen a Face • Landslide • More Than Words • Patience • Redemption Song • Summer Breeze • To Be with You • Toes • Wish You Were Here • and many more.
00001518 P/V/G $19.99

THE MOST REQUESTED BROADWAY SONGS

And I'm Telling You I'm Not Going • Aquarius • Can You Feel the Love Tonight • Corner of the Sky • Getting to Know You • Everything's Coming Up Roses • I Enjoy Being a Girl • It's Delovely • New York, New York • On My Own • Part of Your World • People • Seasons of Love • The Impossible Dream • Til There Was You • Tomorrow • What I Did for Love • and more.
00001557 P/V/G $19.99

THE MOST REQUESTED CHRISTMAS SONGS

Blue Christmas • Christmas Time Is Here • Deck the Hall • Feliz Navidad • Grandma Got Run over by a Reindeer • Have Yourself a Merry Little Christmas • I'll Be Home for Christmas • Jingle Bells • Little Saint Nick • Nuttin' for Christmas • Rudolph the Red-Nosed Reindeer • Silent Night • Wonderful Christmastime • and more.
00001563 P/V/G $19.99

THE MOST REQUESTED CLASSIC ROCK SONGS

Africa • Bang a Gong (Get It On) • Don't Stop Believin' • Feelin' Alright • Hello, It's Me • Layla • The Letter • Life in the Fast Lane • Maybe I'm Amazed • Money • Only the Good Die Young • Peace of Mind • Small Town • Space Oddity • Tiny Dancer • Walk Away Renee • We Are the Champions • and more!
02501632 P/V/G $19.99

THE MOST REQUESTED COUNTRY SONGS

Cruise • Don't You Wanna Stay • Fly Over States • Gunpowder & Lead • How Do You Like Me Now?! • If I Die Young • Need You Now • Red Solo Cup • The Thunder Rolls • Wide Open Spaces • and more.
00127660 P/V/G $19.99

THE MOST REQUESTED FOLK/POP SONGS

Blowin' in the Wind • City of New Orleans • Do You Believe in Magic • Fast Car • The House of the Rising Sun • If I Were a Carpenter • Leaving on a Jet Plane • Morning Has Broken • The Night They Drove Old Dixie Down • Puff the Magic Dragon • The Sound of Silence • Teach Your Children • and more.
00110225 P/V/G $19.99

THE MOST REQUESTED JAZZ STANDARDS

All the Things You Are • Blue Skies • Embraceable You • Fascinating Rhythm • God Bless' the Child • I Got Rhythm • Mood Indigo • Pennies from Heaven • Satin Doll • Sentimental Journey • Someone to Watch over Me • Stella by Starlight • Summertime • The Very Thought of You • What'll I Do? • You'd Be So Nice to Come Home To • and more.
00102988 P/V/G $19.99

THE MOST REQUSTED MOVIE SONGS

Alfie • Born Free • Chariots of Fire • Endless Love • The Godfather (Love Theme) • Goldfinger • I Will Always Love You • James Bond Theme • Mrs. Robinson • Moon River • Over the Rainbow • The Rainbow Connection • The Rose • Stand by Me • Star Wars (Main Theme) • (I've Had) the Time of My Life • Tonight • The Wind Beneath My Wings • and more!
00102882 P/V/G $19.99

THE MOST REQUESTED PARTY SONGS

Another One Bites the Dust • Brown Eyed Girl • Celebration • Dancing Queen • Electric Slide • Get down Tonight • Girls Just Want to Have Fun • Hot Hot Hot • I Gotta Feeling • In Heaven There Is No Beer • Limbo Rock • The Loco-Motion • Shout • Twist and Shout • and many more.
00001576 P/V/G $19.99

THE MOST REQUESTED POP/FOLK SONGS

Alison • Annie's Song • Both Sides Now • The Boxer • California Girls • Fire and Rain • Joy to the World • Longer • Son-Of-A-Preacher Man • Summer in the City • Up on the Roof • and many more.
00145529 P/V/G $19.99

THE MOST REQUESTED WEDDING RECEPTION SONGS

Celebration • Father and Daughter • Have I Told You Lately • How Sweet It Is (To Be Loved by You) • Hungry Eyes • I Gotta Feeling • I Will Always Love You • In My Life • Isn't She Lovely • Last Dance • Let's Get It On • Love and Marriage • My Girl • Sunrise, Sunset • Through the Years • Unforgettable • The Way You Look Tonight • Y.M.C.A. • and more.
02501750 P/V/G $19.99

THE MOST REQUESTED HITS OF THE '60s

Aquarius • The Beat Goes On • Beyond the Sea • Can't Take My Eyes off of You • Do You Want to Dance? • Goldfinger • Good Morning Starshine • Happy Together • Hey Jude • King of the Road • Like a Rolling Stone • Save the Last Dance for Me • Son-Of-A-Preacher Man • These Eyes • Under the Boardwalk • Up on the Roof • and more.
00110207 P/V/G $19.99

THE MOST REQUESTED SONGS OF THE '70s

Ain't No Sunshine • Bohemian Rhapsody • Bridge over Troubled Water • Desperado • Hello, It's Me • I Will Survive • Just the Way You Are • Let It Be • Midnight Train to Georgia • Night Moves • Rocky Mountain High • Summer Breeze • Time in a Bottle • Without You • You're So Vain • Your Song • and many more.
00119714 P/V/G $19.99

THE MOST REQUESTED SONGS OF THE '80s

Africa • Billie Jean • Can't Fight This Feeling • Come on Eileen • Every Breath You Take • Every Rose Has Its Thorn • Faith • Footloose • Hello • Here I Go Again • I Love Rock 'N Roll • Jessie's Girl • Like a Virgin • Livin' on a Prayer • Open Arms • Rosanna • Sweet Child O' Mine • Take on Me • Total Eclipse of the Heart • Uptown Girl • and more.
00111668 P/V/G $19.99

THE MOST REQUESTED SONGS OF THE '90s

All I Wanna Do • ...Baby One More Time • Barely Breathing • Creep • Fields of Gold • From a Distance • Livin' La Vida Loca • Losing My Religion • MMM Bop • My Heart Will Go On (Love Theme from 'Titanic') • Semi-Charmed Life • Smells like Teen Spirit • 3 AM • Under the Bridge • Who Will Save Your Soul • You Oughta Know • and more.
00111971 P/V/G $19.99

SEE YOUR LOCAL MUSIC DEALER OR CONTACT:

 cherry lane music company

 EXCLUSIVELY DISTRIBUTED BY
HAL•LEONARD CORPORATION
7777 W. BLUEMOUND RD. P.O. BOX 13819 MILWAUKEE, WI 53213
Prices, content, and availability subject to change without notice.

0615